WHAT ARE THEY SAYING ABOUT
MORAL NORMS?

What Are They Saying About Moral Norms?

Richard M. Gula, S.S.

TH
11
GU-WH

PAULIST PRESS
New York/Ramsey

Acknowledgments

Excerpts from *Casti Connubii, Address to Midwives, Humanae Vitae,* and *Human Life in Our Day* are reprinted from Odile M. Liebard, ed., *Official Catholic Teachings: Love and Sexuality* (Wilmington, N.C.: McGrath Publishing Co., 1978). Reprinted by permission of McGrath Publishing Company. Excerpts from *Pacem in Terris, Populorum Progressio, Octogesima Adveniens* are reprinted from Vincent P. Mainelli, ed., *Official Catholic Teachings: Social Justice* (Wilmington, N.C.: McGrath Publishing Co., 1978). Reprinted by permission of McGrath Publishing Co. Excerpts from James M. Gustafson, *Christ and the Moral Life* (New York: Harper and Row, 1968; reprint edition Chicago: University of Chicago Press, Midway Reprint, 1976) are reprinted by the permission of University of Chicago Press. Excerpts from Richard A. McCormick, "Moral Norms and Their Meaning," are reprinted from *Lectureship* (St. Benedict, Oregon: Mount Angel Abbey Press, 1978). Reprinted by the permission of Mount Angel Abbey Press. The diagrams for Strict Consequentialism and Deontological Approach are adapted from Howard Brody, *Ethical Decisions in Medicine*, first edition (Boston: Little, Brown and Co., 1976); second edition, 1981. Adapted by permission of Little, Brown and Co. The diagram of the structure of moral theology has been adapted from the doctoral dissertation of Charles M. Swezey, *What is Theological Ethics? A Study of the Thought of James M. Gustafson* (Ann Arbor: University Microfilms Intl., 1978). Used by permission of Charles M. Swezey.

Imprimatur
+ Most Rev. John R. Quinn
  Archbishop of San Francisco

February 13, 1981

The *Imprimatur* is an official declaration that a book or pamphlet is free of doctrinal or moral error. No implication is contained therein that anyone who has granted the *Imprimatur* agrees with the contents, opinions or statements expressed.

Library of Congress
Catalog Card Number: 81-83188

ISBN: 0-8091-2412-2

Published by Paulist Press
545 Island Road, Ramsey, N.J. 07446

Printed and bound in the
United States of America

Contents

Preface

After some two decades of intensive activity by professional moral theologians, the quest for a renewed moral theology remains unfinished. The state of moral theology today is marked by incompleteness, tentativeness, probing strategies of moral reflection, and significant diversity. The source, meaning, and limits of moral norms are among the most important and controversial areas of contemporary moral theology.

Moral norms are the criteria of judgment about the sorts of persons we ought to be and the sorts of actions we ought to perform.

The discussion of moral norms is inseparably connected with other serious moral concerns such as the range of interest that makes up the field of moral theology, the context in which moral theological reflection occurs, the use of Scripture and natural law in moral reflection, the episcopal moral magisterium and the use of authority, the formation of conscience and pastoral guidance, to name but a few. These concerns have attracted a great deal of attention in recent moral literature, especially among Catholics. This book will give a report on some of this literature, principally the Catholic literature, in an effort to clarify the directions which the discussion of moral norms is taking.

Discussions about moral norms also frequently raise questions about the existence of permanent and enduring moral norms. Are there any moral absolutes? Yes, indeed there are. Official documents of the papal and episcopal magisterium witness to them and the consensus of theologians endorses that witness. At times, however, affirming absolutes can have the unwanted side effect of creating the impression that all norms are absolute. They are not. Yet showing that not all are absolute can often create the impression that there are no absolutes. But there are. Simple alternatives—either all norms are absolute or none are—will not suffice. The discussion which tries to sort out the difference is complex. Therein lies the task of this book. It is intended to be a work of exposition that will try to set forth as clearly as possible the directions of the current discussion among theologians on moral norms. "Directions" is about all we can hope for at this stage in a discussion that is very active, complex, and incomplete.

In order to bring some focus to the directions of a complex discussion on moral norms, I will address five questions: (1) What is the relation of moral norms to the message of Jesus and to the broad range of interests that make up moral theology? This will be an effort to situate moral norms within an understanding of the Christian moral life and the components of moral reflection. (2) What is the context for the contemporary discussion of moral norms? This will be an attempt to describe the philosophical and theological shifts that have occurred in recent times to make the discussion of moral norms so lively. (3) What is the source of moral norms? This calls for a consideration of Scripture and the meaning and use of natural law in relation to moral norms. (4) What are the meaning and limits of moral norms? This will explore the types of moral norms and be the proper context for understanding the meaning of absolutes. (5) Practically, what place do moral norms have in pastoral guidance? This will identify some of the pastoral implications of the pluralism on moral norms in moral theology today.

Like all of theology, and like good moral decisions, this book is the result of broad consultation and the help of many people with different perspectives. I want to thank those good people. During the months spent in writing this book, I have been encouraged and greatly helped by discussion about its contents with many colleagues and friends who took time to read all or significant parts of it along the way. I wish to give special recognition and thanks to my Sulpician colleagues: Frs. Howard Bleichner, Peter Chirico, Ron Chochol, Jerry Coleman, Phil Keane, and Larry Terrien, and to other colleagues and friends: Frs. Tim Kidney and Steve Rowan, and Mr. George Weigel.

1
Moral Norms and Moral Theology

Two dangers lurk in the woods of the discussion of moral norms. One is that a discussion of moral norms can get so philosophical that it seems to be far removed from the message of Jesus. We can too easily forget that the moral life is a response to God in Christ and through the Spirit. A second danger is that we can too readily identify moral norms with the whole of moral theology and expect moral norms to carry the full weight of our moral analysis and subsequent moral choice. We need to see clearly how a discussion of moral norms fits into the message of Jesus and the complex whole of moral theology.

Moral Norms and the Message of Jesus

The core of Jesus' message and ministry is the kingdom (or reign) of God. The Gospel of Mark summarizes the whole of Jesus' message this way: "This is the time of fulfillment. The reign of God is at hand! Reform your lives and believe in the Gospel" (Mk. 1:15). Thus, Jesus' message is an announcement calling for a response. The whole moral life is a response to a call, to the divine initiative. Call-response forms the structure of the moral life in the message of Jesus, though nowhere does Jesus, or the New Testament at large, provide a moral system as such. This does not mean that Jesus' message and ministry make no demands on us or are divorced from moral behav-

5

ior. Rudolf Schnackenburg's still valuable work, *The Moral Teaching of the New Testament,*[1] helps us understand Jesus' fundamental moral message.

The kingdom of God is the love of God holding sway over our life. Where we have been grasped by this love and respond to it, there is the kingdom of God. The sayings of Jesus about the kingdom (see especially Lk. 11:20; 17:20–21; Mt. 11:12) show there is some tension between the present and future in Jesus' understanding of the kingdom. The time of fulfillment, identified by Mark, has not yet completely arrived. The kingdom is present and yet still in the future. The kingdom is present in the person of Christ, his words and saving deeds (like healings and exorcisms), but not yet present in all its peace, power and glory.

This tension between the present and future kingdom provides a fertile source of moral obligation. Jesus' parables of the kingdom challenge us to re-examine our accepted norms of behavior and basic attitudes and values. The parables of the kingdom turn our world upside down and challenge us to reconsider our perspective on life and our posture in the world (see, for example, The Good Samaritan in Lk. 10:30–37, The Friend at Midnight in Lk. 11:5–18, The Wedding Guest in Lk. 14:7–11, The Rich Man and Lazarus in Lk. 16:19–31, and The Pharisee and the Publican in Lk. 18:10–14). The kingdom is promised only to those with a certain posture and perspective toward life (Beatitudes in Mt. 5:3–12), and they who show an active love of neighbor inherit the kingdom (Mt. 5:38–48; 25:31–46). Jesus also insisted on special demands for those who associate themselves in closer discipleship with him and with the kingdom (Mk. 10:1–31; Mt. 19; Lk. 9:57–62).

The fundamental demand made by Jesus on those who wish to share in the kingdom was that they should repent, or convert. Conversion (*metanoia*) calls not just for an inner attitude of regret and sorrow, but for turning away from a way of life now recognized as wrong and setting out in a new direction. Conversion expresses itself in conduct, in works of love (see The Penitent Woman in Lk. 7:36–50).

Closely associated with the demand of conversion are other demands Jesus makes upon those who wish to share in the fullness of the kingdom. Among these are faith, baptism, and good works that exemplify the turning around of one's life. The demand to be a "disciple" expresses most powerfully the fullest expression of conversion. The call to discipleship is the call to the imitation of Christ (Jn. 13:15), to be as Jesus was, to act on his behalf, to preach his message and exercise his powers in his name, even to share in his very destiny (Mk. 8:34–35; Lk. 22:28–30; Jn. 12:26).

The moral life of discipleship is a life turned around by conversion, focused on the kingdom, and expressed in love. The most unambiguous demand Jesus makes on his disciples is to respond wholeheartedly to his commandment of love[2] (Mt. 22:34–40; Mk. 12:28–34; Lk. 10:25–28). In laying down the double commandment of love, Jesus linked and put into mutual relation the love of God and the love of neighbor. The love of God finds expression in the love of neighbor, and the love of neighbor receives its foundation and energy in the love of God. Rudolf Schnackenburg expresses clearly what Jesus did by linking these two commandments of love:

> He revealed the indissoluble interior bond between these two commandments; he showed clearly that the whole law could be reduced to this and only this chief and double commandment, and he reinterpreted "neighborly love" as "love of the nearest person," that is, he interpreted it in an absolutely universal sense.[3]

Jesus showed us through his own life, and most especially by his death (1 Jn. 3:16), what loving God and your neighbor as yourself can mean in concrete reality. Jesus remains the model of love, the norm of the Christian moral life. (For this reason, we will return to Jesus as the norm of the moral life at the end of this book.)

Jesus taught us by his life and continues to teach us through the Spirit what love demands. But we still face a problem. How are we supposed to follow Jesus' example and respond to him and his command of love in our vocations as wives and husbands, mothers and fathers, priests and religious, single men and women, young people and children? It is not easy to say. Following Jesus, that is, being his disciple, does not mean imitating him by being condemned by the Sanhedrin or being nailed to a wooden cross by Roman soldiers.

Rather, following Jesus means, at least, living our human adventure as authentically as he lived his.

We are helped in this effort not only by the testimony of moral witnesses (and thus the need for the lives of the saints in our moral life and teaching), but also by the formulation of moral norms. While the Spirit continues to be the inner law enabling us to imitate and embody the love of Christ, the formulation of moral norms helps us to translate and transmit the Spirit's bidding through the ages. Following Jesus' example of love in the general orientation of our life is hard enough; expressing that love in particular actions is even harder. Moral norms that have been discovered and formulated by those sensitive to the Spirit's lead through the ages help us very much.

The commandment "You shall love your neighbor as yourself" has been the foundation stone for much of the debates in the effort to renew moral theology or explain the so-called "new morality." The primacy of love has long been recognized for its unique role in relating a person to God and to others in a unifying fashion.[4] The effort to formulate moral norms is an effort to bring the meaning and demands of the Christian response of love to moral situations. Moral norms participate in an effort to make meaningful the love which Jesus commanded.

Moral Norms and Moral Theology

How does a discussion of moral norms fit into the whole of moral theology? Many people still mistake a discussion of moral norms for the whole of moral theology or, at least, for the whole process of moral analysis and decision-making. But this is not as it should be. Moral norms are indeed a significant component of moral theology, but not the whole of it. Also, moral norms are indeed relevant to any moral decision but not the sole consideration in coming to a moral verdict.

We can appreciate the particular place moral norms have in moral theology and in moral decision-making if we answer two questions: What constitutes the range of interest for moral theology? What basic points need to be considered in the moral decision-making process? One of America's leading Protestant ethicians, James M. Gustafson of the University of Chicago, has written several books and articles which help us see clearly the whole of moral theology and moral decision-making.[5] I will rely on his structure and method to situate this discussion of moral norms.

Moral Theology

Moral theology, or Christian ethics, is concerned with God's revelation of himself in Christ and through the Spirit as an invitation calling for our response. In short, moral theology is interested in the implications of Christian faith for the sorts of persons we ought to be (this is often called "the ethics of character" or "agency ethics") and the sorts of actions we ought to perform (this is often called "the ethics of doing"). Both concerns—character (or agency) and action—need to be considered in any complete project of moral theology. While this book will try to show how moral norms relate to both character and action, it will not be a complete project in moral theology. This is because a discussion of moral norms does not say all that needs to be said about moral theology. What else is there?

Professor Gustafson has made some clear distinctions that help us see what else there is. He speaks of moral theology, or Christian ethics, as a relationship of theory and practice, or more specifically, *ethics* and *morals*.[6] An example shows their interrelationship. At the level of practice (*morals*), the norm (life is sacred and ought to be respected) gives a reason for an action (no abortion). The level of theory (*ethics*) tries to give some support to the meaning and use of this norm in practice. Since this book is primarily a discussion at the level of *ethics,* I want to explain what Gustafson means by the two tasks that make up moral theology.

Ethics, in Gustafson's terms, is the theoretical part of moral theology. This means it is a level of thinking that is prior to action and serves as the basis for answering the practical question, "What should I do?" According to Gustafson, *ethics* is made up of three formal elements: (1) an understanding of the human person as a moral agent; (2) an understanding of the good as the goal of moral conduct; (3) points of reference (like moral norms) which serve as criteria for moral judgment.[7]

Morals, in Gustafson's terms, is the practical level of moral theology. *Morals* is concerned with answering the practical question,

"What should I do?" Answering this question involves at least four tasks according to Gustafson: (1) analyzing the situation in which the moral dilemma arises—this involves a careful gathering of data in order to get the lay of the moral land; (2) knowing the specific character of the moral agent who must decide and act in this situation—this involves a consideration of the agent's capacities, dispositions, intentions, and the like; (3) considering the agent's basic religious beliefs and fundamental convictions—these influence the interpretation the agent makes of the moral situation and the direction the agent takes in life; (4) appealing to appropriate norms—this enlightens and guides the agent in order to ensure that significant values are properly respected.[8]

Professor Gustafson's understanding of the structure of moral theology can be diagramed as is indicated in Figure 1.[9] The lines show the relationships of theory and practice. Solid lines indicate direct relationships; dotted lines indicate other possibilities. Most of the time, limited relationships are at issue. Such is the case in this book. Its interest can be diagramed like this:

Professor Gustafson's analysis is useful because it shows that moral norms are indeed an integral part of the whole of moral theol-

Figure 1

MORAL THEOLOGY

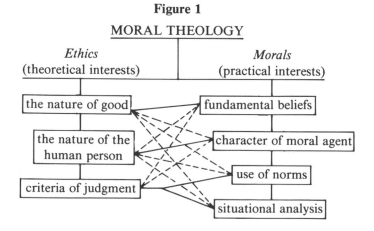

ogy and a relevant, though limited, component in the process of reaching a moral verdict.

Notes

1. *The Moral Teaching of the New Testament* (New York: Herder and Herder, 1965).

2. *Ibid.,* especially pp. 90–109. See also the more recent work on the love commandment by Victor Paul Furnish, *The Love Commandment in the New Testament* (Nashville: Abingdon Press, 1972).

3. *The Moral Teaching of the New Testament,* p. 95.

4. We need only to recall the influence of that significant work which bore a great influence on the pre-Vatican II renewal of moral theology: G. Gilleman, *The Primacy of Charity in Moral Theology* (Paramus: Newman Press, 1959).

5. Gustafson's two most significant books which illustrate the structure and interrelationship of parts in the field of ethics are *Christ and the Moral Life* (New York: Harper and Row, 1968; reprint edition Chicago: University of Chicago Press, Midway Reprint, 1976), and *Can Ethics Be Christian?* (Chicago: University of Chicago Press, 1975). For a succinct article on this distinction, see "Theology and Ethics" in *Christian Ethics and the Community* (Philadelphia: United Church Press, 1971), pp. 83–100.

6. "Theology and Ethics," in *Christian Ethics and the Community,* p. 85.

7. See especially *Christ and the Moral Life,* pp. 1–4.

8. Three articles by Gustafson in which these four base points appear, although in slightly different form, are "Moral Discernment in the Christian Life" in *Theology and Christian Ethics* (Philadelphia: United Church Press, 1974), pp. 99–119; "Context Versus Principles: A Misplaced Debate in Christian Ethics" in *Christian Ethics and the Community,* pp. 101–126; and "The Relationship of Empirical Science to Moral Thought" in *Theology and Christian Ethics,* pp. 215–228.

9. This diagram is adapted from the doctoral dissertation of Charles M. Swezey which examines the correlations more extensively, *What Is Theological Ethics? A Study of the Thought of James M. Gustafson* (Ann Arbor: University of Microfilm International, 1978), pp. 26–33, see especially p. 30. Used by permission.

2
The New Context for Moral Norms

New things are happening in moral theology, especially in the discussion of moral norms: new ideas, new language or concepts for expressing ideas new or old, new methods, new conclusions. All of this can easily be confusing, discouraging, or even threatening. And so understanding contemporary theology requires reaching behind the changes that strike us immediately to get hold of the "why" behind the "what" of these changes. When we do this, we discover that shifts in the understanding of three areas have greatly affected the discussion of moral norms. These areas are (1) the knowledge of reality—what do we know and how? (2) worldview—what is the point of view of contemporary theology? (3) method—what approach does contemporary theology take in deriving moral norms?

The Knowledge of Reality

"Morality is based on reality"[1] is a fundamental axiom operating in the Catholic tradition in its approach to moral norms. This axiom raises questions that take us to the heart of the discussion of moral norms. These questions are basic questions pertaining to our knowledge: How do we know reality? What can we know? How reliable is our knowledge?

The differences in moral methods and moral positions today are often traceable to differences not in a theory of ethics, but in a cognitional theory.[2] The relationship between reality and our capacity to know it can get us involved in very complex cognitional theories. This is not the place to get so involved. Bernard Lonergan has already explored these complexities with great precision.[3] I will rely on his analysis and sketch those features of his position which show that our capacity to know reality is the root issue in the development of thinking on moral norms.

How Do We Know?

1. *Experience.* Experience is the beginning of knowledge. Our capacity to know reality is analogous to my experience of coming to know Mount Rainier. For three years I lived in the Puget Sound area where Mount Rainier is referred to simply as "the mountain." Only about a two-hour drive from downtown Seattle, the mountain stands majestically over the city and the Puget Sound area. Looking at the mountain from Highland Drive's Carey Park on Queen Anne Hill, one can give a general description of the size, shape, and color of the mountain which is accurate, but limited to what one can know of it from Carey Park. But as anyone knows who has been lured to Mount Rainier itself, the knowledge we have of it from the city is certainly not knowledge of the whole of the mountain. What we do have, however, is a sufficient grasp of the whole to urge us to move on to discover more.

I have been lured to the mountain many times with many different kinds of people. Each person who has been to the mountain with me has had a different experience of it. Some have experienced the mountain in its giant glaciers and rock formations carved by glacier action. Others experience the mountain in its meadows and trees. Still others experience it in its milky white streams of glacier run-off, or in its cool, crisp, fresh air. My friends of a more theological sort experience it as "inspiring awe" or as manifesting God's mighty power in creation.

Experience tells me that the knowledge I have is based on something that is really out there. But looking at what is out there and seeing it are only the first operations in the knowing process; they take place at the level of "experience." Through experience we gather data; that's all, nothing more.

2. *Understanding.* Gathering data is not enough to satisfy the desire to know. We want to know more than data. We want to "understand" the data, to "see into" it. Understanding is called forth by the question "What is it?" Understanding puts the separate parts of the data into some kind of order so that we can grasp the whole of what is given in the data. To understand, to answer the question "What is it?" we begin to sift through the data, to walk around it and look at it from all different sides (like the mountain). We look at it in all its relationships. In going through this process we come to what Lonergan calls "insight": a new way of seeing what we first experienced just by looking. We are beginning to "know" the mountain. We have moved from the first level ("experiencing") to the second: "understanding."

3. *Judgment.* There is another step, another operation in the knowing process. We are not yet satisfied. Understanding raises another question, "Is it so?" This is the question of adequacy, of truth. We want to have some assurance that what we have "looked at" and "understood" is true. Does our understanding reflect reasonably what the mountain is? This is the operation of making what Lonergan calls "judgment." In this operation we try to ask as many questions as we can about our understanding so that we may come to as accurate a judgment as possible.[4] Only with the achievement of this critical judgment is knowledge of reality, in its proper sense, attained. It is from this knowledge that we move on to deciding and acting.

In raising questions about our experience, understanding, and judgment, we are all wrapped up with the object we are trying to understand. This means that we have no true grasp of reality apart from being involved in it. There is no way to separate the "knowing subject" from the "object known." The very process by which we have come to knowledge and truth has so involved us in a relationship with the object that we can no longer be separated from it. That is why we cannot really have "objectivity" apart from a relationship to "subjectivity."[5] We either get to "know" reality, and so get caught up in a relationship with what we are trying to know, or we just do not *know* at all. We just take a look and move on.

What Do We Know?

Through experience we gather data, and through our understanding and judgment we try to account for as much data as possible. But the accounts of our experience, understanding, and judgment do not catch the whole of reality at once. Grasping the whole is something like fishing. We have to throw the line in many times before we have a catch. This means that we have many experiences, create many accounts, or formulate many hypotheses. Each of these needs to be tested. We are constantly refining our hypotheses or formulations in order to give a better account of the data.

To make progress toward truth, we must make observations of the data and be free of preconceived notions that control from within our understanding of the data. One bias that might prevent our grasping what is true is reflected in those famous seven last words, "We've never done it that way before." Such an attitude can block us from ever seeing a new set of relationships or being open to a new kind of experience.

When we have an accurate grasp of reality and assent to truth by an accurate judgment, we want to rest in it. But this rest stop, this partial yet reliable grasp of truth, is less like a comfort station and more like a launching pad. We have not yet arrived at the whole of reality or truth, but we have reached a new point of departure. Lonergan's cognitional theory as well as the sociology of knowledge clearly shows us that the whole is bigger than any partial grasp of it or of our effort to give an account of it.[6] The search for the whole goes on. New experiences bring new data which require revision of our previous grasp of reality.

A new experience, a journey farther up the mountain, or even to the other side, may force us to review the process by which we came to our former conclusions, as well as the conclusions themselves. In this review, we may discover that we missed some clues, or that we have new ones. We may also recognize that we allowed foreign elements to enter in and contaminate our analysis, or we may see that we were not all that free from blinding prejudices. Also, dissenting voices with thoughtful contrary opinions may cause us to reconsider our account and give attention to the truth grasped by another's contribution. All of these lead to a necessary revision of our former accounts, formulations, or conclusions. But once we realize that we do not grasp the whole of reality through any one experience, or express it in any one formulation, we should not be surprised that much of what we know remains open to revision. The process of knowing is an ongoing one.

The Knowledge of Reality and Moral Norms

This theory of how we know and what we know has important implications for moral theology. One important implication is the interpretation of "objectivity" in morality. Lonergan's cognitional theory shows that there is a significant place for the subject (the person) in the process of grasping the meaning of reality. Moral theology today is overcoming the dualism of the subject-object split by giving significant attention to the role of the person in moral action and to the experiences of moral persons in the formulation of moral norms. With both physical things like mountains, and with moral issues like taking life, we tend to identify what we see as "objective" knowledge. We readily equate the "objectivity" of knowledge with what is out there to be seen.[7] According to Lonergan's theory, this is not quite correct. "Objectivity" is not the thing "in itself." "Objective" knowledge is not what we know by looking. This is true in the moral world as much as in the physical world.

For example, in morality we often want to locate "objective" morality in the physical structure of an act, such as inserting a knife into a living body. On the other hand, we want to identify "objective" morality with some norm of conduct, such as "Do not take the life of an innocent person." However, neither the physical act nor the behavioral norm expresses the objective moral reality. If we think they do, then we have stopped too soon and have committed the common fallacy in moral thinking of substituting a part for the whole.

Some contemporary moral theologians see that moral action cannot be designated "objectively" moral or immoral (i.e., intrinsically evil) until action, intention, and circumstances are taken into consideration *simultaneously*.[8] Objectivity is understood in a relational rather than in a physical way. Walter Jeffko suggests the metaphysical basis for this position in this statement:

> It is a widely held view in contemporary metaphysics that reality is fundamentally "processive" and "relational" rather than static and thing-like. From Hegel onward, this has been the prevailing metaphysical view of reality, not to mention the profound influence of both physical and biological science.[9]

Furthermore, contemporary moral theology does not separate the development of moral norms from the experience of values important to the full development of human life.[10] Our knowledge of these values at any one time is by no means exhaustive. We continue to seek their meaning. While the knowledge of values at any one time may be accurate and reliable, it is also partial. While we have genuine insight into these values, our formulations never succeed in capturing all the intricacies and complexities of what these values demand. These limitations on our knowledge and our ability to express what we know call for some humility in our theological discussions and a necessary tentativeness in the formulations of our moral norms.

Moreover, contemporary theology recognizes that everyone is involved in this journey of coming to truth. The episcopal magisterium[11] plays an indispensable role in this journey. The episcopal magisterium is like our reliable, trustworthy guide up the mountain. But even the best guides need assistance. In a climbing party, everyone has a responsibility for the climb. And so it is in theology. All teach and all learn. Everyone contributes according to his or her own proper competence, while respecting differences in authority and responsibility.[12] Mutual sharing in the teaching-learning process is how we climb together toward a more complete grasp of truth. We are always on the way to a fuller grasp of truth. We need the collaboration of various perspectives, different experiences, years of testing, raising new questions, coming to a rest stop, and launching on ahead. Our greatest danger is to stop too soon and to claim too much for too little.

Worldview

When I try to explain what is meant by a "worldview" and the shift in worldviews, a clip from *Peanuts* comes to mind. Linus is struggling with his introduction to new math. In his frustration he exclaims, "How can you do 'new math' problems with an 'old math' mind!" Linus has it exactly right. The issue is his "worldview" (also called "point of view" or "consciousness"). Something like the old math/new math shift has occurred in theology.

Bernard Lonergan helps us understand the shift from the old theology to the new theology when he speaks of the shift from the "classicist" worldview to one marked by "historical conscious-ness."[13] The Age of the Enlightenment marks the beginning of this shift; the development of empirical science and philosophy's "turn to the subject" were major influences. These movements called into question the great conceptual systems of well-defined essences ex-pressed in abstract, universal concepts. The impact of these move-ments and the shift in worldviews has been strongly reflected in the theology of Vatican II and in subsequent theological discussion.

Classicist Worldview: Static Essences

Stated briefly, the classicist worldview works on the assumption that the world is a finished product. Everything is done; nothing new is to be added. The classicist worldview mistakes knowing for look-ing. One only needs to look upon the world to discover its order. A good look grasps·immutable essences which yield a high degree of certitude and can be stored up to remain valid forever. An implica-tion for living is that there is nothing more to do but reproduce the order given in the world and to live by it. The Greek Parthenon and the Gothic cathedrals are symbols of the classicist worldview. Each represents a world standing in well-balanced proportions. Stability is the principal virtue; change is a threatening vice. Abstract, universal, eternal, necessary, essential, and static are adjectives that character-ize the classicist worldview.

Modern Worldview: Historical Consciousness

The modern, historically conscious worldview sees all things as part of a whole. Life is an ongoing process of knowing more and more. For the historically conscious worldview, thinking in evolutionary terms is quite natural. The historically conscious view conceives the person as part of an ongoing process that allows us to grow closer to the truth but not to be so bold as to claim the whole of it anywhere along the way. This point of view recognizes that all knowledge is conditioned by time and place, limited self-awareness, and limited grasps of reality. Concrete, individual, and changing are adjectives that characterize this point of view. Change, development, and revision are not signs of imperfection, but are ways of coming to the truth. This point of view believes we come to possess truth slowly, but that we do have reliable places to rest along the way. We are not constantly wandering aimlessly with nothing to give us direction. Our rest stops are reliable grasps of truth that launch us on the way to new discoveries.

Worldviews and Moral Theology

The shift of worldviews has been reflected in the theology of the Vatican II documents and in subsequent theological reflections. The *Pastoral Constitution on the Church in the Modern World* is an excellent example. It can make its clarion call to "read the signs of the times" with some credibility because the document itself recognizes that "the human race has passed from a rather static concept of reality to a more dynamic, evolutionary one" (n. 5). Other signs in modern theology that reflect this shift in worldviews are the frequent appearance of the fundamental ideas of a readiness for change, the need for development, the courage to take risks based on limited knowledge, the centrality of conversion, and the openness to reformulating long-standing principles. This openness to the need for reformulation is clearly affirmed in the 1973 document *Mysterium Ecclesiae* of the Doctrinal Congregation. This document shows that the historical conditioning of formulations and the possible need for reformulation has now been accepted officially by the episcopal magisterium.[14]

The accompanying chart sketches some prominent features of both worldviews. There are many dangers inherent in laying out so cleanly the differences in the two worldviews. For instance, there is really no "pure" classicist worldview or modern worldview which can serve as a paradigm for these differences. Furthermore, there is no single person or document that can be unambiguously identified with either worldview. There are many different types of each worldview and different degrees to which persons and documents reflect them.

The ongoing revision of Catholic moral theology today is an effort to incorporate the insights and advantages of the modern, historically conscious worldview while not ignoring the perduring values of the classicist worldview. Contemporary moral theology

FEATURES	CLASSICIST WORLDVIEW	MODERN WORLDVIEW
A. Characteristics	Views reality primarily as static, immutable and eternal	Views reality primarily as dynamic and evolving, historical and developing
	The world of reality is marked by objective order and harmony	The world of reality is marked by progressive growth and change
	Speaks of the world in terms of well-defined essences and abstract, universal concepts	Speaks of the world in terms of individual traits and concrete, historical particulars
B. Method	Begins with abstract, universal principles	Begins with the experience of the particular
	Primarily deductive	Primarily inductive
	Conclusions always the same	Some conclusions change as the empirical evidence changes
	Conclusions are always secure and complete as long as deductive logic is correct	Leaves room for incompleteness, possible error; open to revision; conclusions are as accurate as evidence will allow

FEATURES	CLASSICIST WORLDVIEW	MODERN WORLDVIEW
C. Moral Theology and the Moral Life	Deals with issues in the abstract and as universal	Deals with issues in the concrete particularity of historical moment
	Deals with universals of humanhood	Deals with the historical person in the historically particular circumstances
	Conforms to pre-established norms and to authority	Formulations of norms are historically conditioned
	Emphasis on duty and obligation to reproduce established order	Emphasis on responsibility and actions fitting to changing times
	Lacks integration with the great mysteries of faith and roots in critical biblical orientation	More soundly integrated with the mysteries of faith and nourished by biblical teaching
D. Advantages	Clear, simple, and sure in views of reality and in its conclusions about what ought to be done	Respects the uniqueness of the person and the ambiguities of historical circumstances
		Sees the moral life as always incomplete and in need of conversion
E. Disadvantages	Tends to be authoritarian in the sense of claiming to have answers suitable for all time	Tends to relativism in the sense that nothing seems unconditionally binding
	Tends to be dogmatic in the sense of having the last word	Tends to be antinomian in the sense that all laws are irrelevant

wants to preserve the clarity, consistency, and precision of the classicist worldview while at the same time respecting human freedom, the uniqueness of the historical moral situation, and the unfinished character of the moral life so valued by the historically conscious worldview. Contemporary moral theology is not a matter of "either/or," either classicism or historical consciousness. As Richard P. McBrien points out, the relationship of classicism and historical consciousness in contemporary theology is one of dialectical tension.[15] That is to say, there are values in both approaches that should not be ignored.

However, McBrien also points out that there is perhaps one irreconcilable difference between the two worldviews: "The classicist assumes that one can know and express absolute truth in ways that are essentially unaffected by the normal limitations of our human condition."[16] Because the classicist rejects in principle the assertion that the perception and expression of truth is historically conditioned, moral theology cannot follow classicism alone in its formulation and use of norms. Classicism would be generally indifferent to the sociology of knowledge and the findings of the empirical sciences as well as the impact of ongoing experience on the meaning and limits of moral norms. And yet, moral theology today cannot follow historical consciousness alone, for that would underestimate the impact of norms to provide continuity and stability in the moral life and to counter tendencies toward subjectivism and relativism in moral matters. Catholic moral theology today respects continuity and discontinuity.

Method

The third shift behind the changes in the discussion of moral norms is that of method. Contemporary theology's method is reflected in Vatican II's *Pastoral Constitution on the Church in the Modern World.* Before beginning its second part which gives its reading of the signs of the times, the document states its methodological preference in an introductory paragraph saying that it is going to consider the urgent needs of the present age "in the light of the Gospel and of human experience" (n. 46). This statement tips the document's hand showing its favor for a more historically conscious inductive method in theology.

What is this method like? Perhaps a study in contrasts will show its points of emphasis. The moral manuals, the standard seminary textbooks which were in vogue up to Vatican II, reflect the classicist worldview. Their method is deductive. The classicist worldview presumes that we can have a clear grasp of the essence of reality, human nature, and the human good in a clear and distinct way. With universal, abstract essences as the starting point, deduction yields concrete material norms that would be applicable always, everywhere, and for everyone. Abstract essences of human nature and moral action formed the basis of universally applicable and unexceptionable moral norms. This leaves little room for taking seriously historical development, uncertainty, the complexities of human existence, or being tentative about norms and their application.

The historically conscious worldview of modern moral theology supports a method that is empirical and inductive. This is not to say that deductive reasoning has no place in modern moral theology. It still does. But moral theology today is more likely to begin with historical particulars, the concrete, and the changing.[17] It is reluctant to draw conclusions independently of a consideration of the human person and the complexities of human existence. This requires a greater concern for the developmental, personalist, and social structural dimensions of lived experiences. In order to gain access to this experience, the social sciences must form an integral part of the reflection on complex moral dilemmas.

What are some of the implications of the inductive method for moral theology? One implication addresses our expectations of moral norms. Since the inductive method gives such significant attention to the concrete and the historical, we can no longer expect our behavioral norms to spell out everything in advance. To think that they did or could do so would be to take our hospital code of ethics as the sure answer to all the doctor's dilemmas, or it would make our norms of social justice determine all the statesman's verdicts.

Furthermore, an inductive method is reluctant to attribute an "absolute" quality to concrete behavioral norms. While we may all be committed to the same basic values of life—the dignity of the person, health, integrity, justice, or friendship, for example—we do not automatically know what action is always consistent with those values. While we may all agree that we ought to be loving, we may not be able to agree on what being loving in this situation of conflict would be. The inductive method does not bring us to moral conclusions with the unambiguous, comfortable clarity we might wish to have. (Part of the whole problem with any discussion on moral matters is that we want absolute certainty where we cannot get it.)

An inductive method also requires moral theology to pay attention to contributions from the empirical sciences and from the testimony of people of good will. We cannot formulate adequate norms apart from considering empirical data, the data of human experience. The very structure of the knowing process demands it. In moral matters, experience is a valid source of moral knowledge about the human good and a valid source for confirming moral judgments.[18] This means that we ought to pay closer attention to the experience of the moral community and the consequences of what helps and what hinders the full development of human life in the process of formulating and interpreting moral norms.

Greater appeal to the empirical sciences and to the experience and testimony of people of good will affects the way we formulate new norms and assess past ones. For example, some matters about which we have made unambiguous moral judgments in the past (such as masturbation, contraception, sterilization, religious liberty, and usury) are now seen to be much more complex realities than our formulations admitted. The appeal to empirical data and the testimony of people of good will softens the severity of some of our formulations and weakens their claims for certain, universal application. The inductive method is, in many ways, forcing us to bring the ancient and honorable prudential process closer to center stage.

Furthermore, an inductive method encourages the teaching-learning process of coming to truth. The conclusions of an inductive method do not claim to be absolutely certain and free from error. An inductive method accepts limitations of conclusions based on the possibility of limited evidence and insight. Mistakes are the way to fuller understanding. A dissenting opinion becomes new data to be interpreted, evaluated, and appropriated for its kernel of truth. The inductive method requires that its conclusions are, at best, tentative summaries of the present state of the question. An inductive method does not claim to solve completely a problem or close a discussion. It always remains open to new experience and insight because it proposes its conclusions as identifying the way things appear to be at the present time.[19]

Further significance of the way we know and what we know, wordview, and method on moral norms will be evident in the chapters ahead. The purpose of this chapter has been to paint in broad strokes three significant shifts affecting the discussion of moral norms today.

Notes

1. Daniel C. Maguire has explored the implications of this axiom to great benefit for understanding how to do ethics. See *Death by Choice* (Garden City: Doubleday and Co., 1974), especially Chapter Four, pp. 77–114. See also his *The Moral Choice* (Garden City, Doubleday and Co., 1978), especially Chapter Five, pp. 128–188, though the whole book is rooted in this axiom.

2. John G. Milhaven raised some important questions of epistemology for ethics in the early days of the debates on the renewal of moral theology. See his "Toward an Epistemology of Ethics," *Theological Studies* 27 (June 1966): 228–241. This was reprinted in *Norm and Context in Christian Ethics,* edited by Gene H. Outka and Paul Ramsey (New York: Charles Scribner's Sons, 1968): 219–231; also reprinted as "Criticism of Traditional Morality" in Milhaven's book, *Toward a New Catholic Morality* (Garden City: Doubleday, 1970): 127–139. More recently, Milhaven has continued to show the significance of epistemology for ethics in his "Objective Moral Evaluation of Consequences," *Theological Studies* 32 (September 1971): 407–430; also, "The Voice of Lay Experience in Christian Ethics," *CTSA Proceedings* 33 (1978): 35–53. John P. Boyle has provided two articles which also show the significance of epistemology as a basic issue for ethics in "Faith and Christian Ethics in Rahner and Lonergan," *Thought* 50 (1975): 247–265; also, "The Natural Law and the Magisterium," *CTSA Proceedings* 34 (1979): 189–210.

3. Lonergan's most extensive treatment of his cognitional theory is in *Insight* (New York: Philosophical Library Inc., 1957); a more succinct treatment is in his essay "Cognitional Structure," *Collection,* edited by F. E. Crowe (New York: Herder and Herder, 1967): 221–239.

4. This tries to capture the sense of Lonergan's notion of coming to a "virtually unconditioned judgment" which is a key notion in his epistemology. See the short section, "The General Form of Reflective Insight" in *Insight,* pp. 280–281.

5. This position is evident in Lonergan's epistemology. See, for example, the reflective study of John P. Boyle, "Lonergan's *Method in Theology* and Objectivity in Moral Theology," *Thought* 37 (July 1973): 599–601. This understanding of the relationship of "objectivity" to "subjectivity" is also confirmed by the sociology of knowledge. See, for example, Werner Stark, *The Sociology of Knowledge* (London: Routledge and Kegan Paul, 1967); also, see Peter Berger and Thomas Luckmann, *The Social Construction of Reality* (Garden City: Doubleday, 1967).

6. *Ibid.* The sociology of knowledge has helped us realize that our knowledge is limited by where we stand (intellectually, socially, geographically, or otherwise). Our knowledge changes as we move from one place to another. But since we cannot see reality from all points of view at once, we must remain open to a revision and expansion of our knowledge.

7. Bernard Lonergan distinguishes two disparate meanings of the term "object," and two different criteria of "objectivity". "Object" can refer to the world of immediacy or to the world mediated by meaning. In the world of immediacy, the criterion of objectivity is the proper functioning of our senses. In the world mediated by meaning, the criteria of objectivity are the data of sense and of consciousness, the operations of intelligence and reasonableness, and the result of combining these two. Lonergan concludes: "For it is now apparent that in the world mediated by meaning and motivated by value, objectivity is simply the consequence of authentic subjectivity, of genuine attention, genuine intelligence, genuine reasonableness, genuine responsibility. Mathematics, science, philosophy, ethics, theology differ in many manners; but they have the common feature that their objectivity is the fruit of attentiveness, intelligence, reasonableness, and responsibility": *Method in Theology* (New York: Herder and Herder, 1972), pp. 262–265, quotation at p. 265. An attempt to rethink the meaning of moral objectivity by giving significant place to the subject has been evident in the work of Stanley Hauerwas. See his *Character and the Christian Life* (San Antonio: Trinity University Press, 1975), *Vision and Virtue* (Notre Dame: Fides Publishers, Inc., 1975), *Truthfulness and Tragedy,* co-authored with Richard Bondi and David B. Burrell (Notre Dame: University of Notre Dame Press, 1977), and *A Community of Character* (Notre Dame: University of Notre Dame Press, 1981).

8. This has been expressed most articulately by Josef Fuchs, "The Absoluteness of Moral Terms," in *Readings in Moral Theology No. 1: Moral Norms and Catholic Tradition,* edited by Charles E. Curran and Richard A. McCormick (New York: Paulist Press, 1979): 94–137, at p. 121.

9. "Processive Relationism and Ethical Absolutes," *ibid.,* p. 199.

10. This understanding of moral norms is expressed most clearly by Daniel C. Maguire, *The Moral Choice,* especially Chapter Seven, pp. 218–260.

11. The designation "episcopal magisterium" is used deliberately. It shows that the teaching function of the Church is a shared responsibility. The teaching function is not exclusive to the bishops, although the bishops do have a special place in the teaching function of the Church. This special designation is inspired by a quotation like the following which captures well the spirit of shared responsibility for teaching in the Church: "Despite an unfortunate modern use of the word *magisterium* to designate the bishops, the college of bishops, and the Pope, magisterial authority is not confined in the Church to official magisterial authority. It cannot reasonably be maintained, in the face of Vatican II, that the Church is divided into an *ecclesia docens* consisting of the Pope and the bishops and an *ecclesia discens* embracing all other baptized persons. On the contrary, everyone in the Church, from the Pope downwards, belongs to the 'learning Church' and has to receive information and enlightenment from his fellow-believers; and everyone in the Church who has reached maturity has, at some time or another, to play the role of teacher, the *magister,* the *ecclesia docens*": B. C. Butler, "Authority and the Christian Conscience," *The Clergy Review* 60 (January 1975): 3–17, at p. 13. For a recent discussion of the "senses" of magisterium, see Avery Dulles, "Doctrinal Authority for a Pilgrim Church" in *The Resilient Church* (Garden City: Doubleday, 1977), pp. 93–112, especially pp. 104–107. Also, see Dulles, "The Magisterium in History: A Theological Reflection," *Chicago Studies* 17 (Summer 1978): 264–281. This whole issue is a valuable summary of present-day discussions on the magisterium.

12. In recent years, theologians have frequently spoken of the inseparability of the teaching-learning function of the Church. For a few examples, see Richard A. McCormick, "The Magisterium and Theologians," *CTSA Proceedings* 24 (1969): 239–254; also his "Moral Notes," *Theological Studies* 29 (December 1968): 714–718; and 30 (December 1969): 644–648; also, his "The Contemporary Moral Magisterium," *Lectureship* (St. Benedict, Oregon: Mount Angel Abbey Press, 1978): 48–60.

Some documents of Vatican II have also witnessed to the importance of drawing upon different competencies in coming to truth. See especially *Gaudium et Spes,* n. 62, which advocates not only freedom of inquiry but also the need for all who search for truth to share resources and points of view proper to different areas of competence. *Lumen Gentium,* n. 37, encourages ongoing dialogue between the laity and clergy for the sake of promoting the mission of the Church and sharing in the apostolate of the hierarchy.

The 1976 statement of the International Theological Commission, "Theses on the Relationship Between the Ecclesiastical Magisterium and Theology," acknowledges that both bishops and theologians have a teaching function in the Church, although it is realized in different ways and with different kinds of authority (see Theses 1–9). Also, this statement clearly advocates fulfilling the common task of defending the certainty of faith in a co-responsible, cooperative, and collegial way (Theses 10 and 11). These *Theses* were issued June 6, 1976 and are available as a USCC publication, 1977.

13. See Bernard Lonergan, "Theology in Its New Context," *Theology of Renewal,* Vol. 1: *Renewal of Religious Thought,* edited by L. K. Shook (New York: Herder and Herder, 1968), pp. 34–46; also his "The Transition from a Classicist World-View to Historical Mindedness," *Law for Liberty,* edited by James E. Biechler (Baltimore: Helicon Press, 1967): 126–133; also, his "Dimensions of Meaning," in *Collection,* pp. 252–267.

14. See Appendix for the relevant citation from this document.

15. *Catholicism,* Vol. 2 (Oak Grove: Winston Press, 1980), p. 942.

16. *Ibid.,* p. 943.

17. For a more thorough analysis of these contrasts, see Charles E. Curran, "Absolute Norms in Moral Theology," *Norm and Context in Christian Ethics,* pp. 139–173, especially pp. 166–173. More recently, see his "Natural Law," in his own collection of essays, *Themes in Fundamental Moral Theology* (Notre Dame: University of Notre Dame Press, 1977): 27–80.

18. John G. Milhaven has consistently been urging that more attention be given to experience and empirical evidence in moral matters. See note 1 above. Also, Daniel C. Maguire has shown the significance of individual and group experience as a valid source of knowledge for making a moral choice. See his *The Moral Choice,* especially Chapter Ten, pp. 309–342.

19. The use of the inductive method to promote the teaching-learning process of coming to moral truth has been a consistent theme of Richard A. McCormick. See, for a few examples, the selections identified in note 11 above.

3
The Sources of Moral Norms

Roman Catholic theology has traditionally identified two sources of moral norms: Scripture and natural law. We will consider briefly what theologians are saying about each.

Scripture

The function of Scripture in moral theology is a delicate and difficult issue. While we have some very significant works that study the moral teaching in the Bible,[1] we do not yet have comparable works that show us how to use the Bible in our moral teaching.[2] However, from the seminal work that has been done on this issue, we can get a preliminary sense of the attitude of contemporary theology toward Scripture as a source of moral norms.

The biblical renewal in the Catholic Church has indeed made its impact on moral theology. The efforts at renewing moral theology made by Bernard Häring and Charles E. Curran, for example, show this quite well.[3] Their writings have made it clear that Christian morality is a religious morality. This means that the Christian moral life is the expression of one's relationship to God manifest in and through one's relationship with others. This has helped arouse the social consciousness of our moral thinking. Furthermore, the biblical renewal has given to moral theology and to the moral life its basic structure of call-response: God takes the initiative to call us into relationship with him; we are free to respond to God in and through our responses to the persons and events that make up our life. The moral life can be understood in this way as the response to the word and work of God manifest in and through Christ and the Spirit. This call-response structure makes the moral life primarily a "vocation" characterized by "responsibility." The biblical notion of "covenant" provides the overarching context for this understanding of the moral life.

Moreover, the biblical renewal has contributed to the person-centered thrust of contemporary morality by stressing the significance of the heart. The "heart" in the biblical sense is the very center of the person, the source of all thoughts, values, desires, and decisions. Also, the emphasis in contemporary morality on growth, development, and creativity as marks of the moral life over passive conformity to law has roots in the biblical renewal, especially with the attention given to covenant, conversion, and kingdom in biblical theology.

The biblical renewal has ended the manual's practice of turning to Scripture as an arsenal of proof texts for positions taken on other grounds.[4] We recognize today the historical and cultural limitations of biblical teaching which prevent applying Scripture in a timeless manner to different historical circumstances. We must travel the long road of interpretation to move from the biblical text to moral teaching.

Two methodological questions on the relationship of Scripture to moral theology can bring what is at issue into focus. Charles E. Curran has identified them well.[5] The first asks, "Is there a distinctive method for Christian morality?" The general consensus among Catholics and Protestant theologians is that there is not.[6] Christian morality shares the method of ethics in general. (Figure #1 in Chapter One shows the formal elements of ethics in general and their possible relationships.) This heightens the difficulty of knowing just what Scripture contributes to morality. This difficulty has not been resolved, but something of what is at stake emerges here in the explicit attention given to the second question.

The second question asks, "Is there distinctive content to Christian morality at the level of moral conclusions, proximate values, and norms?" In the midst of ethical and religious pluralism, as well as in the face of historical evidence that Christian morality has not cornered the market on morally superior people, the relation of Christian morality to human morality has taken on a new cast. We can see this through a quick survey of some recent literature.

A growing number of studies among Roman Catholic authors indicate that at the level of concrete, behavioral norms there is nothing distinctive about Christian morality with its appeal to Scripture that could not be discovered by the use of reason. Bruno Schüller argues that all scripturally described moral actions are in principle subject to rational defense. He argues further that natural morality and revealed morality are not really different. The moral imperatives are the same.[7] Josef Fuchs favors a position that regards Christian morality at the level of content to be fundamentally human morality.[8] Richard McCormick has argued similarly that the morality drawn from Christian sources is in principle available to reason and applicable to all people. He says:

Christian ethics does not and cannot add to human ethical self-understanding as such any material content that is, in principle, strange or foreign to man as he exists and experiences himself.[9]

Charles E. Curran holds a similar position. For him the Scriptures cannot be used as a book of revealed morality. The Scriptures do allow the Christian to explicitly reflect on the Christian self-understanding with all the attitudes, goals, values, and norms that ought to accompany such an understanding. However, he says:

The ethical wisdom and knowledge portrayed in the scriptural experience remains quite similar to the ethical experiences of all mankind. The primary difference is the explicitly Christian character of the Gospel which will not affect the proximate ethical dispositions, attitudes and goals as well as concrete conclusions, but will color the explicit self-understanding of the Christian and the decision process he employs.[10]

These conclusions of Roman Catholic moral theologians are supported by a Roman Catholic biblical scholar from Louvain, Raymond Collins. His study of the relation of Scripture to Christian morality comes to five conclusions. First, ethical teaching is an integral part of the Gospel message. Second, the content of the ethical teaching in the New Testament does not come directly from Jesus himself. The authors borrowed from a variety of sources, such as Stoic philosophers, the law, Jewish catechetical material, and the moral sense of the authors themselves. This results in an openness and pluralism in New Testament morality which makes it impossible to reduce the moral teaching of Jesus to a single view. Third, formal norms are given more significance than concrete, material norms. Occasionally material norms (like the prohibition of divorce in Mark 10:11–12) are introduced to implement formal norms (fidelity in marriage), but there is evidence of adding or deleting material norms as circumstances warrant. Fourth, "love" links together the ethical teaching of the various authors, but each approaches love in a different way to show that it must be a personal response to a personal need. Lastly, the moral views of the New Testament authors are presented in a theological context. Since the content is essentially secular, the context brings the distinctively Christian character to New Testament morality.[11]

This discussion is not limited to Catholic theologians alone. Many Protestant theologians have made a contribution as well and, in doing so, are shattering any stereotypes that would want to place all Protestants under the same Reformation principle, *sola scriptura.* John Macquarrie, for example, shares an opinion similar to the Catholic authors cited above. For Macquarrie, Christian morality is distinguished not by its content of goals or norms but by the context within which the moral life is considered.[12] James M. Gustafson has not directly asked the question of distinctiveness in the way the Catholics have, but he seems to hold the position that the Christian does in fact face some different moral obligations and will come to some different conclusions on certain matters precisely because of the Christian's particular commitment to Christ and affiliation with the historical community of the Church with its Scripture and traditions.[13] Apart from the question of distinctiveness, Paul Ramsey has consistently appealed to Scripture to defend love as the basic moral norm.[14] H. Richard Niebuhr has said that Jesus gives no new principles but revealed God, the one to whom we are ultimately responsible.[15]

What are we to make of all this? We can see that the Bible is used in diverse ways in moral theology. For someone like Paul Ramsey, it provides a revealed moral law to govern action. For someone like H. Richard Niebuhr, the Bible is a source of knowledge of God and moral thought develops in relation to what one knows about God (Creator, Judge, Redeemer, etc.). For Macquarrie and many Catholics, the Bible provides the context for the moral life so that moral thought develops in light of biblical themes and symbols like resurrection destiny, sin, creation, hope, and life in Christ.[16] These examples are not exhaustive but they do show the variety of uses that Scripture has in morality.

This brief survey shows that there seems to be general agreement among Protestants and Catholics that Scripture is an authority for moral theology. No one seems to disagree with Vatican II's call that Christian morality ought to be renewed in accord with Scripture (*OT,* n. 16). However, this brief survey shows that there remains some disagreement between Protestants and Catholics, though the lines cannot be so clearly drawn, about what Scripture provides for morality and how we are to move from the biblical text to moral claims.[17] No consensus seems to exist on this issue.

Among the leading Catholic theologians who have addressed the issue of the use of Scripture in morality, there seems to be general agreement that Scripture offers an explicit self-understanding, a specific context for understanding the moral life, and motivation for being moral. Also, among these Catholic theologians there seems to be some agreement that, for the most part at least,[18] Scripture does not add new content in the form of concrete behavioral norms which are not already accessible to reason's reflection on human experience. This accounts for the significant amount of attention that is given to a natural law approach for deriving concrete, material norms. Yet, even the use of natural law is not without biblical authorization. Josef Fuchs has devoted some attention to the biblical basis for natural law in his classic work, *Natural Law: A Theological Investigation.*[19] The biblical basis for natural law gives Fuchs the warrants to claim that even norms derived from natural law are rooted in Scripture.

Bruno Schüller has maintained, however, that even though natural law is authorized by Scripture, natural law is necessary in the first place if we are ever to hear and understand revealed morality.[20] While the dialogue between Scripture and natural law morality continues to go on, it remains difficult to say with any satisfactory precision just what Scripture contributes to the formulation of moral norms and how it does so.

Since natural law has so dominated Catholic moral thought, we need to give a significant amount of attention to what the theologians are saying about natural law as a source of moral norms.

Natural Law

In Roman Catholic moral theology, natural law has played a significant part in establishing moral norms. Natural law has provided the basis for claims to certitude in situations of great ambiguity; it has been the basis for deriving norms applicable always, everywhere, and for everyone, and it has been the means by which to argue for the rightness of particular actions without recourse to specifically religious reasons. Since natural law has played such an instrumental role in our moral theology, we will need to give some attention to the understanding of natural law that lies behind the recent discussions of moral norms.

Natural law is a highly ambiguous notion. In a sense, natural law is neither "natural" nor is it "law." It is not "natural" in the sense that the natural moral law cannot be identified with physical, chemical, or biological laws which try to express the way the natural world works. It is not "law" in the sense that it is not a codified body of precepts that carry sanctions from the legislator. Furthermore, historical surveys of the meaning and use of natural law quickly put to rest any notion that natural law is a single philosophical system that yields a clear and consistent code of conduct.[21]

In Roman Catholic moral theology, God is the ultimate source of moral obligation. This is what we express in the notion of "eternal law." All other laws and moral obligations are derived from the eternal law. The natural law is the human way of participating in the eternal law. However, the way we participate in the eternal law through the natural law has been open to a variety of interpretations.

Throughout history, two interpretations of natural law have dominated. Both have their roots in antiquity. Two Romans, Cicero (d. 43 B.C.) and Ulpian (d. 228 A.D.), represent two interpretations of natural law which have had lasting effect on subsequent developments of natural law theory. Cicero spoke of natural law as an innate power to which we ought to conform. This power is reason, prudential and thoughtful judgment. This interpretation has contributed a central place to reason in the meaning and use of natural law. The jurist Ulpian, on the other hand, contributed a physicalist cast to natural law by defining it as what man shares in common with the animals. Following natural law in this interpretation is living in conformity with the facts of life. Moral obligation and moral norms arise from the physical properties, operations, and goals of the "natural" powers or structures of life.[22]

The tension between these two approaches to natural law can be found in St.Thomas and in subsequent Catholic theology. The ambiguity of Thomas and the subsequent vacillation between observing the "order of nature" and observing the "order of reason" to arrive at moral norms have caused great confusion in Catholic moral thought.[23]

The interpretation of natural law that corresponds to the "order of nature" is what St. Thomas calls "generic natural law" (*ST.* I–II, q. 94, a. 2). In this interpretation, St. Thomas is influenced by Ulpian's notion of *ius naturale* (what man shares in common with the animals).[24] This way of understanding natural law emphasizes human physical and biological nature in determining morality. This suggests a "blueprint" theory of natural law which supports physicalism over personalism. "Personalism" is hard to define with precision but is characterized by placing emphasis on dimensions of the human person and human actions which extend beyond the physical and biological to include the social, spiritual, and psychological dimensions as well. "Physicalism," on the other hand, refers to the tendency in moral analysis to emphasize the physical and biological aspects of the human person and human actions.

Stated boldly, physicalism understands nature as the viceroy of God. The rule of God and the rule of nature are practically one. In nature, God speaks. The structures and actions of nature are the expressions of God's actions on humankind. This understanding has

significant implications for morality. Physicalism discovers criteria
for moral judgment by studying human functions in their natural
(read: "God-given") state before any intervention by the human person. Moral norms are "written in nature." They can be "read off"
the physical properties, operations, and goals of the human faculties
(the faculty of speech is for truth-telling, the reproductive faculty is
for producing life). Moral obligations are fulfilled by conforming human action to the detailed patterns found in nature. An action is immoral because it frustrates the finality of a natural (read:
"God-given") faculty. For example, speaking falsely frustrates the
faculty of speech which is oriented to truth-telling, and contraception frustrates the reproductive faculty which is oriented to the giving of life.

The physicalist interpretation of natural law which dominated
the Catholic moral manuals allows moral positions to be taken without ambiguity in every instance where the physical action is the
same. The traditional prohibitions in sexual and medical moral matters, for example, are based largely on this physicalist interpretation
of natural law.[25] Any violation of the natural order has been regarded
as a very serious offense since violating the natural order is an affront
against God, its author. This helps explain in part why our traditional morality maintained that there is no "light matter" in the area of
sexual morality.

Since the order of nature comes directly from God as its author,
it assumes a priority and superiority over the order of reason which
comes more immediately from the human person. St. Thomas maintains this position in the *Summa* when dealing with the morality of
sexual matters:

> Reason presupposes things as determined by nature . . . so
> in matters of action it is most grave and shameful to act
> against things as determined by nature (*ST.* II–II, q. 154, a.
> 12).

In this section, St. Thomas says that in matters of chastity, the most
serious offenses are those against the order of nature, i.e., those actions which do not fulfill the finality written by God into biological

nature. Louis Janssens has studied this section of St. Thomas carefully to show where such a position leads.

> Sexual activities excluding procreation (Thomas classifies them in an order of ascendent gravity: masturbation, marital contraceptive intercourse, homosexuality, bestiality) are sins against biological nature (*contra naturam omnis animalis*). They are graver than the sins which do not exclude procreation (in ascendent degree of gravity: fornication, adultery, incest), because they go directly against God, the Creator who expresses his will in the biological nature. Therefore, in a certain sense they are even graver than sacrilege.[26]

Following St. Thomas' principle that the most serious actions are those which go against nature, we would have to conclude that masturbation is a more serious violation of chastity than incest, adultery, rape, or fornication (*ST.* II–II, q. 154, aa. 11, 12). Janssens shows that contemporary moralists would not draw such conclusions. A different understanding of "nature" and "natural law" has a lot to do with the different conclusions. Contemporary moralists do not understand nature as prescribing God's moral will. Nature provides the material with which we have to deal in a human way to promote the well-being of human life. We discover what natural law requires by reason's reflection on what is given in human experience.[27]

This manner of deriving moral norms on the basis of the "order of nature" over the "order of reason" and pronouncing specific moral judgments on acts in themselves has found its way into the documents of the episcopal magisterium on sexual and medical moral matters. For example, Pius XI in *Casti Connubii* (1930) says this:

> But no reason, however grave, may be put forward by which anything intrinsically against nature may become conformable to nature and morally good. Since, therefore, the conjugal act is destined primarily by nature for the begetting of children, those who in exercising it deliberately frustrate its natural power and purpose sin against nature

and commit a deed which is shameful and intrinsically vi-
cious.[28]

This same understanding of natural law appears again in Pius XII's
Address to Midwives in 1951:

> Nature places at man's disposal the whole chain of the
> causes which give rise to a new human life; it is man's part
> to release the living force, and to nature pertains the devel-
> opment of that force, leading to its completion. . . . Thus
> the part played by nature and the part played by man are
> precisely determined.[29]

Paul VI carried this understanding of natural law forward in
Humanae Vitae in 1968 by maintaining:

> Nonetheless the Church, calling men back to the obser-
> vance of the norms of the natural law, as interpreted by the
> constant doctrine, teaches that each and every marriage act
> (*quilibet matrimonii usus*) must remain open to the trans-
> mission of life. . . .

> To make use of the gift of conjugal love while respecting
> the laws of the generative process means to acknowledge
> oneself not to be the arbiter of the sources of human life,
> but rather the minister of the design established by the Cre-
> ator. In fact, just as man does not have unlimited dominion
> over his body in general, so also, with particular reason, he
> has no such dominion over his generative faculties as such,
> because of their intrinsic ordination toward raising up life,
> of which God is the principle.[30]

Paul VI also reflects St. Thomas in making the order of nature superior to the order of reason by claiming:

> The Church is the first to praise and recommend the inter-
> vention of intelligence in a function which so closely asso-

ciates the rational creature with his Creator; but it affirms that this must be done with respect for the order established by God.[31]

The strength of the physicalist approach to natural law is that it clearly recognizes the "givenness" of human nature. There is indeed a fixed character of human existence with which humankind must cooperate in promoting the well-being of human life. The weakness of this approach, however, is to mistake the "givens" of human nature as the whole of human nature, or to take the fixed character of human existence as being closed and beyond the control of human creative development. Karl Rahner has captured well the tension between the givenness of nature and human creative capacities in this statement:

> For contemporary man, nature is no longer the lofty viceroy of God, one which lies beyond man's control, but instead has become the material which he needs so as to experience himself in his *own role of free creator* and so as to build *his* own world for himself according to his own laws. Of course, it is true that this material of human creativeness has laws proper to itself which will weigh heavily on man. It is true that this human creativeness consequently subjects itself, whether it likes it or not, to what is alien and given to it; it is not pure creativeness as we acknowledge it of God; it does not come completely from within and it is not simply a law unto itself; it does not evoke matter and form out of nothing, and hence this creativeness of man, which has to deal with the laws of matter, is naturally also in every case a growth in obedience and "servitude" in the face of an alien law . . . but it is creation in knowing, willing and mastering sense, a creativeness which forces nature into its own service.[32]

The physicalist approach to natural law has been criticized on many counts,[33] and has been generally rejected by "revisionist theologians."[34] Typical of the critical reactions to this approach to natural law and the conclusions it yields is this one by the Georgetown philosopher, Louis Dupré, made during the birth control debates of the 1960's:

> Such a way of reasoning about nature contains, I feel, two basic flaws. It confuses man's biological structure with his human nature. And it takes human nature as a static, unchangeable thing, rather than as a principle of development. Man's biological life and its intrinsic laws are but one aspect of human existence.[35]

Charles E. Curran has been consistent in his criticism of the physicalist approach to natural law. His criticisms run along several lines. First, the physicalist approach reflects the naive realism of the classicist worldview. This means that physicalism is based on a static and essentialist definition of human nature, considers change and historical process to be only of secondary importance, and supports a static view of the moral order. Physicalism also gives exaggerated importance to the human physical and biological nature in determining morality and so separates the action from the totality of the moral reality. Physicalism claims too many negative moral absolutes based on the action taken in itself, and does not make room for historical development and the creative intervention of reason to humanize the given patterns of nature.[36]

The revisionist theologians are saying today that the natural law need not assume a static, "blueprint" view of human nature and base moral norms on physical criteria alone. Catholic theology has been involved in a serious critique and revision of the physicalist approach to natural law which predominated the manuals of moral theology and some[37] decrees of the episcopal magisterium. Revisionist theologians today are saying that the natural law is not so closely tied to physicalism and the classicist worldview that it would be misleading to use the natural law in a worldview that takes experience, history, change, and development seriously. The roots of contemporary theology's more historically conscious use of natural law are in the second strain of interpretation of natural law, the order of reason.

The natural law as the "order of reason" is found in St. Thomas as the "specific natural law" (*ST.* I–II, q. 94, a. 2). This means that the human person participates in the eternal law according to the way proper to being human, i.e., according to reason. In this interpretation, reason, not the physical structure of human faculties or actions taken by themselves, becomes the standard of natural law. What is reason? From the Thomistic school, reason (*recta ratio*) is the dynamic tendency in the human person to know the truth, to grasp the whole of reality as it is. This means that we must use observation, research, analysis, logic, intuition, common sense, even a poetic sense, and whatever else would give us a knowledge of the whole of reality. A morality that has reason as its basic standard, then, must be a morality based on reality. When morality is based on reality, the moral person and the moral community must discover and recognize the moral good. Natural law, according to this order of reason interpretation, can be described as *reason's reflection on human experience discovering moral value*. The process of discovery and recognition is the work of the moral conscience.[38] This, in brief, seems to be the fundamental direction that recent trends in interpreting the natural law are taking. Much more attention is being given to the total complexity of reality experienced in its historically particular ways.[39]

In a morality based on the order of reason, the human person is not subject to the God-given order of nature in the same way the animals are. The human person does not have to conform to natural patterns as a matter of fate. Rather, nature provides the possibilities and potentialities which the human person can use to make human life truly human. The given physical and biological order does not provide moral norms; rather, it provides the data and the possibilities for the human person to use in order to achieve human goals. The natural order remains an important factor to consider if the human person is to base moral norms on reality. But the natural order is not to be taken as the moral order. The human person can creatively intervene in a reasonable way to direct the order of nature in a way that would be truly human. The "nature" which reason explores is no longer separated from the total complexity of personal, human reality.[40]

This understanding of natural law has important implications for moral norms. Moral norms based on the order of reason express reason's grasp of reality. Insofar as reality continues to change, moral norms must be open to revision. Insofar as reason's grasp of reality is always partial and limited, moral norms are necessarily tentative. While right reason is the full exercise of our capacity to grasp the whole of reality, the full exercise of reason is limited by individual capacities, emotional involvements that bias the interpretation of data, and cultural conditions that influence one's perspective on reality. All of these factors necessarily place limitations on moral norms and moral judgments. And all these factors lead to more modest claims of certitude than did the physicalist criteria of the order of nature.

The order of reason approach to natural law is evident in St. Thomas when he deals with matters of justice (cf. *ST.* II–II, q. 64), and it has found its place in official magisterial documents on matters of social ethics.[41] Although the great social encyclicals *Rerum Novarum, Quadragesimo Anno,* and *Pacem in Terris* reflect something of a static social order, there is sufficient evidence in them of a move away from the physicalist interpretation of natural law evident in decrees on sexual and medical moral matters to an interpretation of natural law that is based on the prudential use of reason. Consider this brief excerpt from *Pacem in Terris* (1963) as a point of illustration for this shift:

> But the Creator of the world has imprinted in man's heart an order which his conscience reveals to him and enjoins him to obey: *This shows that the obligations of the law are written in their hearts: their conscience utters its own testimony. . . .* But fickleness of opinion often produces this error, that many think that the relationships between men and states can be governed by the same laws as the forces and irrational elements of the universe, whereas the laws governing them are of quite a different kind and are to be sought elsewhere, namely, where the Father of all things wrote them, that is, in the nature of man.[42]

Paul VI reflects a dynamic view of natural law that appeals to the creative intervention of the human person and community into

natural processes to direct them to human fulfillment in his great social encyclical, *Populorum Progressio* (1967):

> In the design of God, every man is called upon to develop
> and fulfill himself, for every life is a vocation. At birth, ev-
> eryone is granted, in germ, a set of aptitudes and qualities
> for him to bring to fruition. Their coming to maturity,
> which will be the result of education received from the en-
> vironment and personal efforts, will allow each man to di-
> rect himself toward the destiny intended for him by his
> Creator. Endowed with intelligence and freedom, he is re-
> sponsible for his fulfillment as he is for his salvation. He is
> aided, or sometimes impeded, by those who educate him
> and those with whom he lives, but each one remains, what-
> ever be these influences affecting him, the principal agent
> of his own success or failure. By the unaided effort of his
> own intelligence and his will, each man can grow in hu-
> manity, can enhance his personal worth, can become more
> a person.[43]

Paul VI also expressed a dynamic view of natural law based on
an order of reason which grounds morality in reality and yields tentative norms open to development in his apostolic letter *Octogesima
Adveniens* (more popularly known as "A Call to Action") in 1971:

> In the face of such widely varying situations it is difficult
> for us to utter a unified message and to put forward a solu-
> tion which has universal validity. Such is not our ambition,
> nor is it our mission. It is up to the Christian communities
> to analyze with objectivity the situation which is proper to
> their own country, to shed on it the light of the Gospel's
> unalterable words, and to draw principles of reflection,
> norms of judgment and directives for action from the social
> teaching of the Church.[44]

A comparison of documents representing the order of nature
approach to natural law with those representing the order of reason
approach shows the two different methods that have been operating
in Catholic moral theology side by side to yield moral norms and

moral judgments. The clear distinctions and line drawing that were possible by using the physicalist criteria of the order of nature approach in sexual and medical moral matters are not present in the areas of social ethics. On the basis of physicalist criteria, Catholic sexual and medical morality has achieved a precision and consistency of moral judgment that is not found in its social ethical documents. The order of reason approach to understanding natural law does not yield the clear unambiguous positions that the order of nature approach does. The tentativeness and ambiguity that characterizes moral judgments in contemporary moral theology can be attributed in part to its making greater appeal to the order of reason strain in the tradition of natural law. Before going on to summarize the leading characteristics of a contemporary approach to natural law, it may be well to summarize what we have seen thus far in the accompanying chart that contrasts the salient features of both approaches to natural law.

While there is not yet a totally systematic treatment of a revised theory of natural law, at least certain key features that would be component parts of such a theory have emerged. Timothy E. O'Connell has outlined them well.[45] We only need to summarize his presentation here. With this brief outline we will be ready to explore the meaning and limits of moral norms.

Real

Natural law asserts that morality is based on reality. Realism stands, on the one hand, in opposition to legal positivism which makes something right because it is commanded. On the other hand, realism stands against a morality based on personal whim whereby one can arbitrarily decide what is right and wrong. The dimension of realism in a natural law theory means that the moral life, ultimately, is not a matter of obedience to law, nor is it a matter of doing whatever you want. The moral life is a matter of doing the good. The moral person and the moral community must discover what is morally good in reality. This is the fundamental thrust of a natural law approach to morality. Moral norms, seen from this basis, are generalized expressions of what the moral community discovers to be the morally good in the community's experience of reality.[46]

TWO STRAINS OF INTERPRETATION OF NATURAL LAW AND IMPLICATIONS FOR MORAL NORMS

FEATURES	"THE ORDER OF NATURE"	"THE ORDER OF REASON"
1. Designation of Moral Norms	"According to Nature"	"According to (right) Reason"
2. Source of Moral Norms	"Written in Nature" God is the author of nature. God-given structures take priority over anything derived from reason.	"Reality" taken in all its complexity. Norms express the prudent use of reason in reason's effort to grasp moral obligations grounded in reality.
3. Knowledge of Moral Norms	Observe the way nature works.	Rational grasp of reality. Reason is expressed through whatever means would help us grasp reality in its fullness.
4. Violation	Any interference with the order designed by God is gravely serious. No "light matter" here.	Acting against what you know to be a true expression of what most fulfills human potential as this can be known through a rational grasp of reality.
5. Examples	*Casti Connubii* (1930) Pius XII's *Address to Midwives* (1951) *Humanae Vitae* (1968) *Humana Persona* (1975)	*Rerum Novarum* (1891) *Quadragesimo Anno* (1931) *Pacem in Terris* (1963) *Gaudium et Spes* (1965) *Populorum Progressio* (1967) *Octogesima Adveniens* (1971)

Experiential (Empirical)

If morality is based on reality, we come to know morality through our experience of reality. This suggests an inductive method for moral theology and an appeal to empirical evidence in our process of deriving moral norms and carrying on moral evaluation.[47] We discover moral value through our reflection on the experience of human reality. The norms of Christian morality reflect the collective experience of the Christian community's experience of what it means to be human. As our norms emerge from our experience of what it means to be human, so are they tested by continued experiences of what builds up and promotes the dignity of human life. All this means that our moral theology must pay close attention to what our experience, past and present, is telling us about what it means to be human.

Consequential

With the "consequential" we are entering an arena of much controversy, especially because "consequences" are often interpreted too narrowly to mean the short run, immediate consequences.[48] Consequences are an important focal point for moral meaning, but consequences *alone* do not tell us what is right or wrong. There is more to the moral reality than consequences. Yet consequences are important considerations in the process of formulating moral norms. The moral community's experience of what helps and hinders the well-being of human life gives rise to moral norms. Our norms then communicate the accumulated wisdom of the moral community's experience of good and evil consequences.[49]

Historical

One of the most frequent criticisms made of traditional natural law theory is that it fails to account for the possibility of change and development. Its static view of the moral order produced universal and immutable norms. In contrast, the historically conscious world-view of contemporary theology has as a central characteristic the reality of change and development. Contemporary theology asks whether we can continue to presume that moral conclusions drawn on the basis of historically conditioned experience and a limited perspective can be equally valid for all times, places, and people. Whereas traditional moral theology grounded natural law norms in the abstract, ahistorical, metaphysical nature of man which it held to be unchanging through the ages, contemporary natural law theory grounds moral norms in the metaphysical nature of the human person concretely realized in various stages and situations of history. Contemporary theology recognizes that it cannot ignore the unfinished, evolutionary character of human nature and the human world. The evidence of experience and the verification by data of the historical sciences are too strong.

The influence of historical consciousness on moral norms is great. Our moral norms must be able to take into account our fundamental capacity for change and development. What has built up human well-being in the past may, or may not, continue to do so in the present or future.[50] The historical component of a natural law approach leaves room for change and development. Moral norms developed from this approach will reflect the tentativeness of historical consciousness and the provisional character of moral knowledge.[51]

Proportional

This last component is introduced to help us answer the practical moral question, "What ought we to do?" At the most fundamental level, we ought to do what is genuinely good, what is most loving, what truly contributes to building up the well-being of human life. Yet we know that we are limited in so many ways—personal capacities and skills, time, freedom, etc. The good we do comes mixed with some bad. Our moral efforts are directed toward trying to achieve the greatest proportion of good to evil. The component of proportionality in natural law tells us that we are doing the morally right thing when we achieve the greatest possible proportion of good over evil.[52] This, in fact, gets to the heart of the Christian virtue of prudence as it comes to us through St. Thomas (*ST.* I–II, q. 61, a. 2). It tells us that moral persons must be able to guide us in our prudential judgments, i.e., in our judgments of proportionality.

This, in brief, is an outline of the salient features of a contempo-

rary approach to natural law. It is rooted in the order of reason interpretation of natural law, and it is consistent with the historically
conscious worldview of contemporary theology. Since this approach
to natural law is not dominated by the physicalism of the order of
nature approach, we cannot expect clear, unambiguous formulations
and applications of moral norms. What is evident, however, is that
Catholic morality today is becoming open to the great complexity of
human, personal reality.   .

Notes

   1. Rudolf Schnackenburg, *The Moral Teaching of the New Testament;*
Ceslaus Spicq, *Theologie Morale du Nouveau Testament,* 2 vols. (Paris: Ga-
balda, 1965); Victor Paul Furnish, *Theology and Ethics in Paul* (Nashville:
Abingdon Press, 1968), also his *The Love Commandment in the New Testament.*

   2. A very helpful effort in this regard is the joint work of a biblical
scholar and an ethician, Bruce C. Birch and Larry L. Rasmussen, *Bible and
Ethics in the Christian Life* (Minneapolis: Augsburg Publishing House,
1976). Some significant articles on this issue are Charles E. Curran, "Dialogue with the Scriptures: The Role and Function of the Scriptures in Moral
Theology," *Catholic Moral Theology in Dialogue* (Notre Dame: Fides Publishers, 1972): 24–64; James M. Gustafson, "The Place of Scripture in Christian Ethics: A Methodological Study," *Theology and Christian Ethics*
(Philadelphia: United Church Press, 1974): 121–145; Edward LeRoy Long,
Jr., "The Use of the Bible in Christian Ethics: A Look at Basic Options,"
Interpretation 19 (April 1965): 149–162.

   3. Bernard Häring's writings are vast and wide-ranging. His early
three-volume work, *The Law of Christ,* was one of the first major works by a
Catholic moral theologian to rethink morality in light of the biblical renewal. His most recent three-volume work, *Free and Faithful in Christ* (New
York: Seabury Press, 1978, 1979, 1981), is an expression of Häring's more
mature thought. This work is not a revision of *The Law of Christ.* Charles E.
Curran, a student of Häring, has followed his teacher's lead in making efforts at renewing moral theology in light of the biblical renewal. Some of his
pertinent articles are "The Relevancy of the Ethical Teaching of Jesus" and
"Conversion: The Central Moral Message of Jesus" in *A New Look at Chris-
tian Morality* (Notre Dame: Fides Publishers, Inc., 1968): 1–23 and 25–71;
"The Relevancy" is reprinted as "The Relevancy of the Gospel Ethic" in
Themes in Fundamental Moral Theology (Notre Dame: Fides Publishers,

Inc., 1977): 5–26; see also his "Dialogue with the Scriptures" in *Catholic Moral Theology in Dialogue,* pp. 24–64.

4. A good example of the proof-text use of Scripture in morality can be found in one of the standard moral manuals of medical ethics, Gerald Kelly's *Medico-Moral Problems* (St. Louis: The Catholic Hospital Association, 1958). After arguing for the prohibition of contraception from natural law and on the basis of the official teaching of the Church, Kelly cites in support of this position the story of Onan (Genesis 38:8–10), pp. 159–160. Modern biblical scholarship does not read this text as a sin of sexual indiscretion.

5. "Dialogue with the Scriptures," *Catholic Moral Theology in Dialogue,* pp. 24–64, especially pp. 47–64.

6. *Ibid.* Also, James M. Gustafson, *Christ and the Moral Life* (New York: Harper and Row, 1968), p. 3.

7. "Zur theologischen Diskussion über die lex naturalis," *Theologie und Philosophie* 41 (1966): 481–503.

8. "Gibt es eine spezifisch christliche Moral?" *Stimmen der Zeit* 185 (1970): 99–112; also "Human, Humanist and Christian Morality" in *Human Values and Christian Morality* (Dublin: Gill and Macmillan, 1970): 112–147.

9. "The Insights of the Judeo-Christian Tradition and the Development of an Ethical Code" in *Human Rights and Psychological Research,* ed. Eugene Kennedy (New York: Thomas Y. Crowell Company, 1975): 23–36, at p. 29; "Notes in Moral Theology," *Theological Studies* 38 (March 1977): 58–70, at p. 69; and "Does Religious Faith Add to Ethical Perception?" *Personal Values in Public Policy,* ed. John C. Haughey (New York: Paulist Press, 1979): 155–173, esp. p. 167.

10. "Dialogue with the Scriptures," *Catholic Moral Theology in Dialogue,* p. 64.

11. "Scripture and the Christian Ethic," *CTSA Proceedings* 29 (1974): 215–241, summary at pp. 240–241.

12. *Three Issues in Ethics* (New York: Harper and Row, 1970): pp. 87–91.

13. Gustafson's position is most thoroughly presented in *Can Ethics Be Christian?* (Chicago: University of Chicago Press, 1975).

14. Paul Ramsey's writing is vast and wide-ranging. On this particular question, see, for example, "The Biblical Norm of Righteousness," *Interpretation* 24 (October 1970): 419–429.

15. *The Meaning of Revelation* (New York: The Macmillan Company, 1941): 114–128. See also his great work, *The Responsible Self* (New York: Harper and Row, 1963).

16. Charles E. Curran has shown how these five biblical themes can be

used as the stance for moral theology in "The Stance of Moral Theology," *New Perspectives in Moral Theology* (Notre Dame: Fides Publishers, Inc., 1974): 47–86.

17. A review of the literature on the various approaches for using Scripture in ethics shows this clearly. See Allen Verhey, "The Use of Scripture in Ethics," *Religious Studies Review* 4 (January 1978): 28–39.

18. Josef Fuchs, for example, once identified some moral obligations that could not be known apart from revelation. He mentions as examples the obligation to love God in a supernatural way, to live in Christ and in grace, and the obligation to believe. See his *Theologia Moralis Generalis,* 2 vols, 2nd ed. (Rome: Gregorian University Press, 1971), Vol. 1, p. 89.

19. Translated by Helmut Reckter and John A. Dowling (New York: Sheed and Ward, 1965), pp. 14–32.

20. "Zur theologischen Diskussion," pp. 481–503.

21. Heinrich A. Rommen, *The Natural Law* (St. Louis: B. Herder, 1947); Yves R. Simon, *The Tradition of Natural Law* (New York: Fordham University Press, 1965), pp. 16–40.

22. Even brief historical sketches of the natural law help to identify these two strains. See, for example, Charles E. Curran, "Absolute Norms in Moral Theology," *Norm and Context in Christian Ethics,* ed. Outka and Ramsey, 140–152; Timothy O'Connell, *Principles for a Catholic Morality* (New York: Seabury Press, 1978), pp. 134–144; Columba Ryan, "The Traditional Concept of Natural Law: An Interpretation," *Light on the Natural Law, An Interpretation,* ed. I. Evans (Baltimore: Helicon Press, 1965), pp. 13–37.

23. Charles E. Curran's work has explored this ambiguity well. For his most recent effort, see "Natural Law," *Themes,* pp. 27–80.

24. This interpretation of Ulpian and his influence on St. Thomas and the subsequent Catholic moral tradition can be found in Curran's survey, *ibid.* See also the more specifically historical essay by Michael B. Crowe, "St. Thomas and Ulpian's Natural Law," *St. Thomas Aquinas 1274–1974: Commemorative Studies,* ed. Armand A. Maurer, 2 vols. (Toronto: Pontifical Institute of Mediaeval Studies, 1974), Vol. 1, pp. 261–282.

25. An excellent book that traces the physicalist interpretation of natural law through Catholic medical ethics in North America was written by David F. Kelly, *The Emergence of Roman Catholic Medical Ethics in North America* (New York: The Edwin Mellen Press, 1979).

26. "Norms and Priorities in a Love Ethics," *Louvain Studies* 4 (Spring 1977): 234–235. References to St. Thomas in this quotation are *ST.* II–II, q. 154, aa. 11, 12 ad. 4; *De Malo* q. 15, a. 1 ad. 7; *ST.* II–II, q. 154, a. 12 and a. 12 ad. 2.

27. *Ibid.,* p. 236.

28. All excerpts from official ecclesiastical documents in this section are taken from the handy resource book, *Official Catholic Teachings: Love and Sexuality,* ed. Odile M. Liebard (Wilmington, N.C.: McGrath Publishing Company, 1978). This quote is on p. 41.

29. *Ibid.,* p. 102.

30. *Ibid.,* pp. 336–337.

31. *Ibid.,* p. 339.

32. "The Man of Today and Religion," *Theological Investigations,* Vol. 6, translated by Karl-H and Boniface Kruger (New York: Seabury Press, 1974), p. 8.

33. See for example, the excellent article by Edward A. Malloy, "Natural Law Theory and Catholic Moral Theology," *American Ecclesiastical Review* 169 (September 1975): 456–469, especially pp. 457–461.

34. "Revisionist theologians" is being used here and throughout this book to refer to those Catholic theologians who are rooted in the Catholic moral tradition, acknowledge its achievements, but are modifying the classical language and method of that tradition. The pacesetters among the Catholic revisionist theologians are such figures as Charles E. Curran, Josef Fuchs, Bernard Häring, Louis Janssens, Peter Knauer, Daniel C. Maguire, Richard A. McCormick, and Bruno Schüller.

35. *Contraception and Catholics: A New Appraisal* (Baltimore: Helicon Press, 1964), pp. 43–44.

36. See Curran's "Absolute Norms in Moral Theology," *Norm and Context,* ed. Outka and Ramsey, pp. 139–173; also "Absolute Norms and Medical Ethics," in Curran's edited collection *Absolutes in Moral Theology?* (Washington: Corpus Books, 1968), pp. 108–153; and his "Natural Law," *Themes,* pp. 27–80.

37. "Some" is an important qualifier because Catholic social encyclicals show a different understanding and use of natural law than do the documents addressing sexual and medical moral matters.

38. X. Colavechio, "Conscience: A Personalist Perspective," *Continuum* 5 (1967): 203–210.

39. Summaries of trends in natural law thinking can be found in Richard A. McCormick, "Moral Notes," *Theological Studies* 28 (December 1967): 760–769; also, George M. Regan, *New Trends in Moral Theology* (New York: Newman Press, 1971): 115–144. For some creative articles on natural law, see those by Curran in note 36 above, also Bernard Häring, "Dynamism and Continuity in a Personalistic Approach to Natural Law," *Norm and Context,* Outka and Ramsey, eds., pp. 199–218; Michael B. Crowe, "Natural Law Theory Today," *The Future of Ethics and Moral The-*

ology, Richard A. McCormick, *et al.* (Chicago: Argus Communications Co., 1968): 78–105.

40. Josef Fuchs, "Human, Humanist and Christian Morality," *Human Values,* pp. 140–147, especially at p. 143.

41. For a study of natural law in the social encyclicals, see Charles E. Curran, "Dialogue with Social Ethics: Roman Catholic Ethics—Past, Present, Future," *Catholic Moral Theology in Dialogue,* pp. 111–149.

42. These excerpts from ecclesiastical documents are taken from the convenient resource, *Official Church Teaching: Social Justice,* ed. Vincent P. Mainelli (Wilmington, N.C.: McGrath Publishing Co., 1978). For this first excerpt, see p. 64. For an interpretation of "imprinted in man's heart" that follows the "order of reason" approach to natural law, see Fuchs, "Human, Humanist and Christian Morality," *Human Values,* pp. 144–147.

43. Mainelli, ed., *Social Justice,* p. 210.

44. *Ibid.,* p. 255.

45. *Principles for a Catholic Morality,* pp. 144–154.

46. Daniel C. Maguire, *The Moral Choice,* p. 220, confirms "realism" in his approach to moral norms.

47. This has been a consistent theme of John G. Milhaven. See the references to Milhaven in note 1 of Chapter Two. Maguire, *The Moral Choice,* pp. 221–222, confirms the empirical grounding of morality and moral norms. Robert H. Springer is another Catholic theologian who has appealed to the empirical grounding for morality. See his "Conscience, Behavioral Science and Absolutes," *Absolutes in Moral Theology?* Charles E. Curran, ed., pp. 19–56. Charles E. Curran has written a valuable article identifying some of the difficulties involved in moral theology's efforts to dialogue with empirical science. See his essay "Dialogue with Science: Scientific Data, Scientific Possibilities and the Moral Judgment," *Catholic Moral Theology in Dialogue,* pp. 65–110.

48. Richard A. McCormick, "Moral Notes," *Theological Studies* 36 (March 1975): 93–100 reviews pertinent literature on the interpretation of "consequences."

49. The issue of how to regard "consequences" is receiving a great deal of attention in the moral literature. In addition to McCormick's "Notes" in the above note, see the balanced treatment of Maguire, *The Moral Choice,* pp. 150–170. Bruno Schüller works out the significance of consequences for understanding ways of grounding moral norms in his essay "Various Types of Grounding for Ethical Norms," *Readings in Moral Theology No. 1,* pp. 184–198. For two essays in this same collection which are negatively critical of consequences, see John R. Connery, "Morality of Consequences: A Criti-

cal Appraisal," pp. 244–266, and Paul M. Quay, "Morality by Calculation of Values," pp. 267–293.

50. John Noonan's work, *Contraception* (Cambridge: Harvard University Press, 1965), shows how historical factors influenced the weight given to competing values in different historical periods. Natural law theory that is historically conscious will be cautious about issuing single, unambiguous answers for all times.

51. This has been a consistent theme of Charles E. Curran in his analysis of natural law. See his works in note 36 above.

52. The idea of proportionality has been receiving a great deal of attention in recent years. For some pertinent articles in the collection edited by Curran and McCormick, *Readings in Moral Theology No. 1,* see Peter Knauer, "The Hermeneutic Function of the Principle of Double Effect," pp. 1–39; Louis Janssens, "Ontic Evil and Moral Evil," pp. 40–93; Richard A. McCormick, "Reflections on the Literature," pp. 294–340. Also see McCormick's monograph, *Ambiguity in Moral Choice* (Milwaukee: Marquette University Press, 1973). This monograph is now available as the first chapter in *Doing Evil To Achieve Good,* Richard A. McCormick and Paul Ramsey, eds. (Chicago: Loyola University Press, 1978), pp. 7–53. The notion of proportionality will be explored further in the next chapter under the consideration of the revisionist approach to the meaning and limits of moral norms.

4
The Meaning and
Limits of Moral Norms

After this long route by way of context and sources, we come to the meaning and limits of moral norms. According to Daniel C. Maguire, moral norms preserve in propositional form the insights of the human experience of value, the experience of what helps or hinders the well-being of persons and of all creation.[1] Moral norms are not recipes for moral action, nor are they the blueprint for present or future moral structures. However, they do enable us to bring some depth and breadth to moral judgment. They also provide some consistency and stability in the moral life. They provide illuminating patterns and common denominators which help us make our way through potential or real moral dilemmas. Moral norms, while never taking the place of our freedom, can help us discern what is right and good.

Moral norms can be positive (give to each his/her due) or negative (do not kill); very general (be good) or quite particular (do not speak a falsehood). In Chapter One, I indicated that moral theology is interested in both the sorts of persons we ought to be (character) and the sorts of actions we ought to perform (action). Moral theology distinguishes two categories of norms depending on whether they relate to character or action. *Formal* (or general) norms relate

to character. *Material* (or particular) norms, also called concrete, behavioral norms, relate to action. In this chapter, we will look at the
meaning and limits of each type.

Formal Norms

Many people often ask if there are any absolutes in contemporary morality. Are there permanent and enduring moral norms? Yes,
there are. The Roman Catholic Church has frequently witnessed to
these absolutes in official teaching. Of the many examples that can be
given of this witness, this statement from *Persona Humana* (the
"Declaration on Certain Questions Concerning Sexual Ethics") of
1975 is typical:

> Now in fact the Church throughout her history has always
> considered a certain number of precepts of the natural law
> as having an absolute and immutable value, and in their
> transgression she has seen a contradiction of the teaching
> and spirit of the Gospel (n. 4).

Many theologians today interpret these kinds of norms as formal
norms. These permanent and enduring norms reflect fixed points to
divine revelation (like Jesus, the kingdom, conversion, the commandment of love, openness to the poor, etc.) and what is universal to humankind (like basic needs of security, acceptance, affection, etc., and
basic goods like life, freedom, etc.). The origin of such norms reaches
below the permutations of culture and different ages. As *Persona Humana* maintains:

> These principles and norms [which pertain to certain fun-
> damental values of human and Christian life] in no way
> owe their origin to a certain type of culture, but rather to
> knowledge of the divine law and of human nature (n. 5).

Yet the concrete expression of these norms and the fundamental
values which they express partake of particular cultures and historical epochs. Timothy O'Connell explains this well when he says for-

mal norms express values which are universal among humankind. While the way of expressing these values may differ among persons and groups, the affirmation of them as constitutive of what it means to be human is universally accepted.[2] Louis Janssens speaks of the implications of the character of formal norms as absolute this way:

> For instance, it will remain true that, always and in all circumstances, we must be just: we ought to be so disposed as to be concerned with the growth of truly human social relationships and structures as well as with the promotion of the possibilities for that purpose.[3]

What these theologians seem to be saying is that while we can and must speak of some moral norms as absolute, these same norms are nonetheless limited by nothing less than the absolute par excellence of Christian faith—the incarnational principle itself.

Many theologians further relate formal norms to the sorts of persons we ought to be. As Louis Janssens puts it, formal norms "assert what our dispositions ought to be."[4] This means that formal norms point to what the animating element of our moral life ought to be. For Timothy O'Connell, they "articulate the inner value-dynamic of the human person."[5] This means that formal norms do not tell us what we ought to do, but bring to a focus the sorts of persons we ought to become, and they exhort, challenge, and encourage us to become that way.[6]

What are some examples of formal norms? The great commandment: love God and love your neighbor as yourself (Mt. 22:37–40; cf. Mk. 12:29–34; Lk. 10:27) and the golden rule: "Whatever you wish others to do to you, do so to them" (Mt. 7:12; Lk. 6:31) are formal norms. Other examples are do good and avoid evil, respect life, be honest, be just, be chaste, be grateful, be humble, be prudent, be reasonable, etc.; expressed negatively, do not be selfish, vain, promiscuous, proud, stingy, merciless, foolish, etc.

These examples of formal norms are expressed in the language of traditional moral virtues when expressed positively, or vices when expressed negatively. There are other expressions of formal norms which are a little more puzzling than these. The more puzzling kinds of formal norms are those which include such terms as: murder, lying, stealing, adultery, blasphemy, genocide, euthanasia, slavery, etc. What makes these kinds of formal norms somewhat puzzling is that they are expressed with "synthetic" terms.

What is the meaning of synthetic terms? Louis Janssens describes synthetic terms as words "which refer to the material content of an action but at the same time formulate a moral judgment."[7] This means that synthetic terms are compact value terms, not simply descriptive terms; that is, they already bear as part of their meaning a moral qualification. For example, "murder" is a morally qualifying term affirming that a killing (a descriptive term) is unjust (an evaluative term); "lie" is a morally qualifying term affirming that a falsehood (a descriptive term) is immoral (an evaluative term); "adultery" is a morally qualifying term affirming that an act of sexual intercourse (a descriptive term) is with the wrong person and for the wrong reasons (evaluative terms).[8]

Therefore, formal norms that use synthetic terms *not only* identify material action, *but also* bear moral evaluation of that action. When an action is finally designated as "murder," "adultery," "genocide," etc., nothing can ever justify the action to make it morally right. This makes norms which use these terms, norms like "do not lie," "do not steal," "do not commit adultery," absolute. These are absolute because they are tautological; that is, they simply tell us that immoral behavior is immoral. Once an action is designated as immoral, it can never be justified. These norms which use synthetic terms do not give us any new information. They simply affirm what we already know. The real issue that remains for the moral person is not to determine whether murder, lying, stealing, adultery, blasphemy, or the like could ever be justified. They cannot. The real issue is how intention and circumstances must be weighed and related in order to count this material act (killing) as immoral (murder). We cannot know which act of killing is murder until we have considered the whole action. Once an act of killing can rightly be defined by the synthetic term "murder," the action is taken as a whole and no further intention or circumstances can justify it. But the proper proportion of the action, intention, and circumstances must be determined before this judgment can be made.[9]

Formal norms, whether expressing ways of being in the language of virtue or with synthetic terms, are limited in that they do not determine the concrete content of what we ought to do. The formal norm "be chaste," for example, describes an inner attitude of ordering our sexuality in such a way that we respect ourselves, others, and the demands of social life. This norm does not, however, tell us which actions embody a chaste disposition in every instance. In like manner, the formal norm "do not murder" does not give us new information about the action of killing. It simply reminds us of what we already know (unjust killing is unjust) and urges us to act on this knowledge.

Even though formal norms do not tell us what to do, they are still quite useful. Timothy O'Connell and Louis Janssens have been emphatic on the importance of formal norms to provide motivation, exhortation, and challenge to do what we already know to be right and good.[10] Timothy O'Connell says it well:

> I do not need only the data, I also need encouragement. I need formulations of my own values, formulations which in their conciseness and directness help me remain faithful to those values. And here is the specific (and very important) function of formal norms. They take the meaning of humanity, with its challenge of intellect and freedom. They apply that meaning to a particular area of human life (for example, property rights). And they declare, in pithy form, what I already know but tend to forget or neglect: Do not steal. By presenting me with that challenge, almost in aphoristic style, formal norms serve me in those moments of human weakness and temptation which are so much a part of our sin-affected situation.[11]

In conclusion, we see that formal norms are absolute in character and motivational in function. They do not give us specific information to answer the practical moral question, "What ought I to do?" Formal norms presume that we know. Formal norms help us to answer the question, "Must I do this or avoid that?" Formal norms remind us of what is good or bad and encourage us to do good and avoid evil.

Material Norms

Formal norms are not the area of greatest controversy in contemporary theology, especially Catholic theology. Material norms are. Material norms relate to the sorts of actions we ought to perform. Material norms attempt to attach formal norms to concrete pieces of behavior—to speech, to killing, to making promises, to sexual conduct, etc. Thus we have material norms like these: entrusted secrets ought to be kept, do not speak falsely, do not kill, do not use artificial means of contraception.

Material norms lead us closer to answering the practical moral question, "What should I do?" Situations of conflict have forced moral theologians to look more closely at the meaning and limits of material norms. Consider these two examples which are typical of the kinds of moral dilemmas that have forced a great deal of rethinking about the meaning and limits of material norms. If a doctor tells the truth to her patient, she may harm the patient's psychic health. If the doctor speaks a falsehood, she may begin to damage the confidence the patient has in her and the doctor may begin to experience a loss of truthfulness in herself. How is the doctor to live with the material norm: Do not speak a falsehood? Or take the case of the married couple who have all the children they can reasonably care for. They cannot enlarge their family without compromising the well-being of their present children. At the same time, the couple feels that fairly regular sexual expression is necessary for the growth and development of their marriage. They do not feel that they can respond adequately to both values and follow the proscription of contraception in *Humanae Vitae*. What do they do?

A survey of the literature on moral norms discloses three distinguishable groups of approaches. Charles E. Curran and Richard McCormick have identified them in similar ways.[12] One group is described as strict consequentialist or strict teleologist. This position, represented by Joseph Fletcher, holds that the moral rightness of all actions is determined solely by their consequences. A second group, represented by the Catholic revisionist theologians, can be described as mixed consequentialist or moderate teleologist. This position holds that consequences play an important part but not the sole role in determining the moral rightness of an action. The third position is described as deontologist. Germain Grisez, William E. May, and Paul Ramsey represent this position which is substantially norm-centered and maintains some actions are wrong independently of consequences.

I will organize this section of the chapter according to these three groups. I give more attention to the revisionist position since that is the one receiving the most attention in Catholic circles today.

Strict Consequentialist—Joseph Fletcher

Joseph Fletcher's position is most clearly expressed in his celebrated *Situation Ethics: The New Morality.*[13] In that book, Fletcher identifies three ways of approaching morality: legalistic—following laws and thereby constraining human freedom; antinomian—being against laws and any form of guidance or human wisdom embodied in laws; situational—discovering the most loving thing in the situation and then doing it.[14] Fletcher follows this third approach.

The attractiveness of this position is that it puts "love" at the center of the moral life. The difficulty with this position is discovering what "love" means and what the "loving thing" to do in a given situation really is. Fletcher answers this difficulty by maintaining that the loving thing in any situation is whatever will bring the greatest good to the greatest number. As Fletcher puts it, the "love" of situation ethics searches for "the greatest amount of neighbor welfare for the largest number of neighbors possible."[15]

In Fletcher's version of situation ethics, the crucial question the moral person faces is not whether a particular action (like telling the truth) produced the greatest good in the past, but whether it will in *this* instance produce the greatest good for the greatest number. About norms or other forms of moral guidance, Fletcher says this:

> . . . he [the situationist] is prepared in any situation to compare them or set them aside *in the situation* if love seems better served by doing so."[16]

The formal norm, "be loving," is the only norm that abides. Fletcher's approach toward norms and the moral rightness of actions in his version of "situationism" is summarized well in these few sentences of his which serve as a fitting conclusion to his approach:

> *Christian* situation ethics has only one norm or principle or law (call it what you will) that is binding and unexceptional, always good and right regardless of the circumstances. That is "love"—the *agape* of the summary commandment to love God and the neighbor. Everything else without exception, all laws and rules and principles and ideals and norms, are only *contingent,* and only valid *if they happen* to serve love in any situation.[17]

Conclusion: The Strategy of Strict Consequentialism

We can appreciate the place moral norms are given in strict consequentialism when we consider the strategy of decision making of this approach. I have diagramed this strategy in Figure 2.[18] We first need to determine possible alternatives for action and then calculate the consequences of each. We assign a value to each set of alternatives plus consequences depending on how much each set contributes to the greatest amount of neighbor welfare for the largest number of neighbors. The correct moral choice, then, is determined on the basis of the alternative that produces the greatest possible value in its consequences.

Mixed Consequentialism—The Revisionist Theologians

I will report these representative examples of Catholic revisionist thinking on material norms in chronological order to show how the discussion has progressed.

1. *Peter Knauer.* Peter Knauer's work represents what may be considered the first step in a new direction for interpreting the meaning and limits of material norms. His major article on moral norms appeared in various forms between 1965–1967.[19]

Peter Knauer makes his contribution to the discussion of material norms through his efforts to reinterpret the principle of double effect. The principle of double effect has been staple ethical fare for

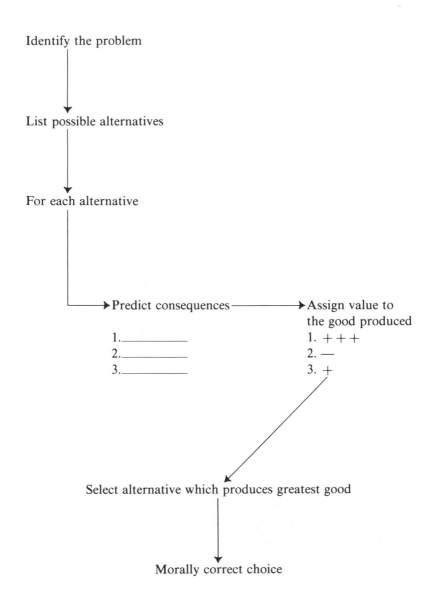

Figure 2
STRICT CONSEQUENTIALISM

centuries in Catholic theology. It helps us through situations of conflict where two values are at stake at the same time and both cannot be preserved. For example, in the case of ectopic pregnancy the life of the mother and the life of the developing fetus are at stake. The principle of double effect helps us to determine whether causing or permitting harm to the mother or the fetus is morally evil. The traditional rendering of the principle of double effect, to put it briefly, assumes that there is a significant moral difference between intending evil and permitting evil as a side effect of a good action. The principle asserts that with a proportionate (commensurate) reason we may permit evil to occur but we may never directly intend to do evil even for a good reason.

Knauer's interpretation of the principle of double effect is this: "The principle of double effect means that to cause or permit an evil without commensurate reason is a morally bad act."[20] His major thesis which has implications for the meaning and limits of material norms reads like this:

> Whether there is a violation of a commandment (that is, whether an act is murder, lying, theft) can be ascertained only if it is established that the reason for the act in its existential entirety is not commensurate.[21]

The key to understanding Knauer's thesis hinges on his distinction between physical evil and moral evil, and on what constitutes a commensurate reason. We need to understand his meaning of each.

Physical evils are such things as sickness, error, destruction, ignorance, loss of reputation, death, or whatever harm we may experience.[22] We do not intend physical evils for themselves but only accept them on account of some associated good which we do want but cannot get apart from taking the physical evil that inevitably comes along with it. Moral evil, says Knauer, "consists in the last analysis in the permission or causing of a physical evil which is not justified by a commensurate reason."[23] Commensurate reason, then, determines to a great extent the moral content of our actions.

When is a reason a "commensurate reason"? And to what is a reason "commensurate"? Knauer is emphatic that a commensurate reason is not just any reason; nor is it simply a serious reason, a sincere reason, or even an important reason.[24] A reason is commensurate for Knauer when there is no long-run contradiction between the value intended and the means of achieving it. Or, to put it another way, a reason for acting is commensurate if causing or permitting some physical evil does not, in the long run, undermine the intended value but actually supports it.[25] Whether a reason for an action is commensurate or not depends on objective criteria and not merely good will.[26] The objective criteria are derived from the proper relationship of three elements: the action, the intention of the agent, and the circumstances in which the action takes place. Since the relationship of these elements cannot be determined in advance, it is not possible to give a catalogue of commensurate reasons for which the act would be regarded as permissible at all times and for which there would be no need for any further considerations.[27]

How does Knauer's thesis work in practice? The practical consequences of his thesis are well illustrated in this example which can serve as a summary of his position:

> Whether the removal of a limb is a health measure or a mutilation of the patient cannot be recognized in the concrete actuality which might be photographed. The reason why the surgeon removes the limb must be looked at. What value does the act seek to serve? It is done because of the health of the patient. But this by itself does not determine the morality of the act. A purely good intention in the psychological sense does not determine the moral goodness of an act. It must be established that this reason is a commensurate one. If, in the given circumstances, the act is the best possible solution of the problem in terms of the horizon given by the whole of reality, it may be said that the act is morally good. In a moral sense, what is then intended is not the taking of the limb, but the health of the patient.[28]

Knauer's analysis has important implications for the meaning and limits of material norms. Should we take material norms as statements of moral qualifications which can be universally applied to particular cases? Knauer says that our norms generally appear to be these kinds of universal statements and receive this kind of application. However, this way of regarding material norms obscures the distinction between physical and moral evil. According to Knauer's position, concrete material norms, especially negative ones, are prohibitions of what causes physical evil without a commensurate reason. For Knauer, "a moral judgment is naturally possible only when in a concrete act it is established whether the reason for the act is commensurate or not."[29] Material norms must not be read as identifying the physical act with the moral order. To prove that the act identified by the material norm is immoral, we must be able to show that this act does not serve the value at stake, but that in the long run it really subverts it. In other words, it must be shown that this particular act does not have a commensurate reason.[30]

2. *Bruno Schüller.* The next significant contribution to the discussion of material norms by a revisionist theologian comes from Bruno Schüller. He tries to find a middle ground between formal norms, which do not specify concretely what we ought to do, and letting the immediate situation alone determine what we ought to do. Schüller's main thesis is this:

> Any ethical norm whatsoever regarding our dealings and omissions in relation to other men or the environment can be only a particular application of that more universal norm, "The greater good is to be preferred."[31]

This thesis expresses Schüller's interpretation of material norms as particular applications of the universal, formal norm "The greater good is to be preferred." Richard McCormick has explained well the meaning of Schüller's "preference principle" which lies behind his interpretation of material norms when he writes:

> Stated negatively, it reads: put in a position where he will unavoidably cause evil, man must discover which is the worst evil and avoid it. Stated positively, this is its formulation: put before two concurring but mutually exclusive val-

ues, man should discover which merits preference and act accordingly.[32]

In light of the preference principle, material norms light up certain values at stake in a situation of conflict. The preference principle limits the application of the material norm by insisting that the norm be followed except in those instances when another more important value is present which deserves preference. This means that there can be exceptions to material norms. Therefore, following in line with Knauer, Schüller would say that we can cause some harm (physical evil) when a greater value demands it.

On what foundation does Schüller rest his position? He explains his theoretical foundation this way:

> Human beings are not in a position to do everything for each other that would be required if everyone wanted to be called good in every sense of the word. The good things which constitute the welfare of a human being can come into conflict with each other, so that the only thing possible is to choose the more important ones.[33]

We only need to recall Knauer's example of the amputation to illustrate this. The injured person must allow his limb to be amputated in order to save his life. Traditionally, theology tried to work out a conflict of values according to the "order of charity" (*ordo caritatis*). This means that what we are to do according to what love requires is worked out by a correct choice of priorities among competing values. For Schüller this happens when we follow the preference principle which says we ought to avoid the greater evil and may do some evil only when necessary for a proportionally greater good.[34]

Schüller illustrates his position with the example of a justifiable exception to the prohibition of killing.[35] The material norm "Do not kill" says that life deserves preference before other co-present values. To make this norm exceptionless would be to say that there is no good thinkable which could conflict with a person's life and which would deserve preference. That traditional theology has made exceptions to the norm against killing in cases of self-defense, just war, and capital punishment shows that we have said there are other goods which deserve preference. While Schüller's position may not alter all traditional conclusions, it does show how all situations of conflict are at least discussable and that material norms are valuable aids to moral choice, even though they are limited ones.

3. *Josef Fuchs.* In 1971 Josef Fuchs wrote a significant article on the issue of "absolutes" in moral norms.[36] For Fuchs the meaning and limits of material norms rest on the distinction between premoral evil (Knauer's "physical evil") and moral evil.[37] Morality, in the strict sense of that term, occurs only in human actions which bear the deliberate decision of the moral agent. This means that the truly moral action is only the one that includes the intention of the moral agent. Particular actions, like driving a car, causing a wound, speaking, or even killing, are not accurately evaluated as moral or immoral apart from consideration of the intention of the moral agent. The most we can say of these actions by themselves is that they are "premoral." Fuchs gives this illustration:

> One may not say, therefore, that killing as a realization of a human evil may be morally good or morally bad; for killing as such, since it implies nothing about the intention of the agent, cannot, purely as such, constitute a human act. On the other hand, "killing because of avarice" and "killing in self-defense" do imply something regarding the intention of the agent; the former cannot be morally good, the latter may be.[38]

Fuchs draws two conclusions which are fundamental to his understanding of the meaning and limits of material norms:

> (1) An action cannot be judged morally in its materiality (killing, wounding, going to the moon) without reference to the intention of the agent; without this, we are not dealing with a human action, and only with respect to a human action may one say in a true sense whether it is morally good or bad. (2) The evil (in a premoral sense) effected by a human agent must not be intended as such, and must be justi-

fied in terms of the totality of the action by appropriate reasons.[39]

This position has significant implications for how we are to judge the morality of an action. Traditionally moralists claimed that certain actions (like contraception, sterilization, masturbation, direct killing of the innocent, divorce and remarriage) were intrinsically evil in themselves. This means that no intentions or circumstances could enter to purify them. The morality of actions was already determined before the person did them in whatever circumstances. To be able to declare an action "intrinsically morally evil" for Fuchs

> ... would presuppose that those who arrive at it could know or foresee adequately *all the possible combinations* of the action concerned with circumstances and intentions, with (premoral) values and non-values (*bona* and *mala "physica"*).[40]

The most we can say about an action apart from considering the intention and circumstances is that this action is good or evil in a premoral sense.

> For (1) a moral judgment of an action may not be made in anticipation of the agent's intention, since it would not be the judgment of a "human" act. (2) A moral judgment is legitimately formed only under a *simultaneous* consideration of the three elements (action, circumstances, purpose), premoral in themselves; for the actualization of the three elements (taking money from another, who is very poor, to be able to give pleasure to a friend) is not a combination of three human actions that are morally judged on an individual basis, but a single human action.[41]

What does all this have to do with the meaning and limits of material norms? Fuchs says that material norms cannot be moral evaluations of actions unless they take into account intentions and circumstances. Without considering all three elements of a moral action, material norms describe actions expressing premoral good or evil. Therefore, there seems to be no possibility according to Fuchs for material norms to describe an action materially (killing) and say that it is always immoral.[42] Material norms light up premoral goods or evils and demand a proportionate reason to cause or permit a premoral evil.

An important implication for the meaning and limits of material norms comes from this position. On this basis, Fuchs concludes that, *theoretically* speaking, there can be no material norm that would be without exception, or "intrinsically evil" in the strict sense. This does not mean, however, that there is no *practical* worth to formulating material norms as universals.[43] Material norms that are practically absolute do point out a value or a non-value in a premoral sense. They indicate that a non-value may be caused or permitted only when urgent values are at stake which deserve preference. Also, certain material norms can be formulated "to which we cannot conceive of any kind of exception, e.g., cruel treatment of a child which is of no benefit to the child."[44] Furthermore, material norms can be stated as universals by a particular culture or society in a particular period of time and "suffice for ordinary use in practical living."[45] These time-conditioned formulations are open to revision as the times change and the conditions which gave rise to the norms change. Material norms for Fuchs, then, are limited, at least theoretically, and so are not without exception. However, in the practical order many material norms function as useful guides to moral behavior with the force of being exceptionless moral norms.

4. *Louis Janssens.* Louis Janssens has contributed what many consider one of the principal moral reflections of our times in his article, "Ontic Evil and Moral Evil."[46] Since Janssens' work is so significant for the contemporary discussion on moral norms, it deserves substantial consideration. This article makes a significant contribution to the discussion of material norms by beginning with a thorough analysis of the structure and the morality of the human act. Janssens does this by returning to St. Thomas, especially his analysis of the structure of the human act (*ST.* I-II, qq. 6–17) and the morality of the human act (*ST.* I-II qq. 18–20). Janssens points out that in Thomas the starting point for understanding human action is the person, especially the end of the inner act of the will, or the intention (*ST.* I-II. q. 8, a. 2; cf. I-II, q. 18, a. 6).

Thomas' view centers on the agent and that *ipso facto* the end of the agent is the fundamental element of the structure of the human act.[47]

Along with the intention, the human act also includes the means-to-an-end (the physical action, or the act-in-itself). The intention of the agent and the means-to-an-end form two structural elements of *one* composite action. To determine the morality of the human action, both of these elements must be taken together. The significance of this is that the physical action itself (the material event, or means-to-an-end) cannot be evaluated morally without considering the actor, especially the intention.[48] This is the position St. Thomas takes in his analysis of what determines the morality of an act (*ST.* I-II, q. 20, a. 3, ad 1). Janssens concludes:

> For this reason [St. Thomas] reacts sharply against those who are of the opinion that the material event of an act can be evaluated morally without consideration of the subject, of the inner act of the will or of the end. As he sees it, an exterior action considered as nothing but the material event (*secundum speciem naturae*) is an abstraction to which a moral evaluation cannot be applied. This object-event becomes a concrete *human* act only insofar as it is directed toward an end within the inner act of the will. Only this concrete totality has a moral meaning.[49]

On these grounds, actions that have the same material features can have different moral meaning depending on the intention which directs the action. For example, making a donation can be morally good when the intention is to bring relief to a person in need. But making a donation can be morally bad if directed by the intention to satisfy one's vanity and win praise.[50] So what is true about the structure of the human act is true about its morality: the formal element, the intention, determines the moral significance of the action.

After showing that the moral goodness of the inner act of the will is the formal element of the exterior act, Janssens shows that St. Thomas argued that "not any kind of exterior action, however, can become the material element of a morally good end."[51] Only an action which is adequately proportionate to the intention can (*ST.* I-II, q. 6, a. 2). But how do we determine what is adequately proportionate? Janssens answers:

> To give an act the character of moral goodness, it is therefore not enough that the end of the subject is morally good: the act is good only when the exterior action (material element, means) is proportionate to the end (formal element) *according to reason,* when there is no contradiction of the means and the end in the whole of the act on the level of reason (*secundum rei veritatem*). Only then is the undivided and composite action morally good, because the means share in the moral goodness of the end within the totality of the act.[52]

The act of self-defense serves to illustrate this. In the case of self-defense, the use of violence (a means-to-an-end) which wounds or even kills the assailant is justifiable when it falls within the limits of what is necessary to save one's own life (the intention). Violence which exceeds the bounds necessary for self-defense is morally evil because this violence (the means-to-an-end) is not proportionate to the intention of self-defense. Therefore causing harm or even death (a means-to-an-end) can be justifiable if it is proportionate to the good intended (the end).[53]

In this example, we can appreciate Janssens' important distinction between "ontic evil" (Knauer's "physical evil" and Fuchs' "premoral evil") and moral evil. The distinction between them and the relation of ontic evil to moral evil are important for understanding Janssens' interpretation of the meaning and limits of material norms.

Ontic evil or, as he speaks of it in another place, "premoral disvalue"[54] is Janssens' way of accounting for the ambiguity of human actions. This ambiguity is the result of the limitations of being human. Ontic evil/premoral disvalue expresses the lack of perfection in anything whatsoever. These notions express limitation, the failure to reach the full actualization of human potential.[55] Ontic evils or premoral disvalues are what we experience as regrettable, harmful, detrimental to full human growth. These would be such things as suffering, injury, fatigue, ignorance, violence, death, etc. Ontic evils are inevitably present in human actions because of the unavoidable limitations that come with being human. As Janssens puts it, ontic evil is present in our actions "because we are *temporal* and *spatial,* live together *with others* in the same *material world,* are involved and act in a *common sinful* situation."[56] This means that we are not able to realize the good without causing or admitting to some ontic evil, or premoral disvalue.

Ontic evil is not moral evil. If these were the same, we could not act morally at all. Moral evil is causing or permitting ontic evil without a proportionate reason.[57] Janssens follows St. Thomas' analysis of the human act again to maintain that there can be no moral judgment of the means-to-an-end (the material element) unrelated to the intention (the end, or the formal element). The moral judgment is a judgment of the proportion of means to end. There is a proper proportion, and the action can be considered moral, when "no intrinsic contradiction between the means and the end may be found in the total act when the act is placed in the light of reason."[58] On this point, Janssens is in line with Knauer by maintaining the axiom of "due proportion" (Knauer's "commensurate reason") as the necessary requirement for judging the morality of the human act. This axiom requires that when we are not able to avoid causing or permitting premoral disvalue (or ontic evil) in our efforts to do good, we must cause or permit the least amount of disvalue possible.

We have already seen this axiom at work in the above example of self-defense. Janssens also makes an application of this axiom to a material norm of marital sexuality:

> According to *Gaudium et spes* the marriage act must be ordered to the conjugal love and to the human transmission of life, viz., to responsible parenthood. This must be the end of marital intercourse; each conjugal act must include a *debita proportio* to this end. Consequently, if the marriage partners engage in sexual intercourse during the fertile period and thereby most likely will conceive new life, the marital act may not be morally justifiable when they foresee that they will not have the means to provide the proper education for the child. The rhythm method, too, can be immoral if it is used to prevent the measure of responsible

parenthood. But the use of contraceptives can be morally justified if these means do not obstruct the partners in the expression of conjugal love and if they keep birth control within the limits of responsible parenthood. Marital intercourse can be called neither moral nor immoral when it is the object of a judgment which considers it without due regard for its end. A moral evaluation is only possible if it is a study of the totality of the conjugal act, viz., when one considers whether or not the conjugal act (means) negates the requirements of love and responsible parenthood (end).[59]

According to this example, we make a judgment that an act is "morally evil" (and therefore "forbidden always and everywhere") too soon if we consider only the external, material act apart from considering the intention of the agent within the given set of circumstances. Therefore, to make a moral evaluation of an action, we must consider the intention of the moral agent and the proportionate relationship of the material action and the intention. If the action does not negate or undermine the basic value intended and if it excludes as much premoral disvalue as possible, then we can say that there is due proportion of means to end and this particular causing or permitting of ontic evil or premoral disvalue is not morally evil.[60] Only when we bring about or permit more ontic evil than necessary to accomplish a good intention is the action immoral.[61] In every situation in which we have to choose between several possibilities, we ought to do that which will contribute as much as possible to the well-being and development of persons and social groups and avoid as much as possible what harms or hinders this well-being.[62]

We can now understand Janssens' interpretation of the meaning and limits of material norms. Because actions must be considered in their entirety (material action, intention, and circumstances taken together), with all the parts in proper relationship, material norms prohibit causing or permitting ontic evils or premoral disvalues without a proportionate reason. As Janssens says:

Briefly, concrete material norms invite us to bring about the ideal relations which lessen more and more effectively all forms of ontic evil which by their definition hamper the development of human beings and communities.[63]

Material norms are not yet moral judgments in the true sense. They would pronounce us guilty of immorality when we do more harm (ontic evil/premoral disvalue) than necessary to achieve good. Material norms do not solve our moral problems, but they do light up premoral values and disvalues and prepare us to exercise prudence. Material norms instruct us on important values (e.g., life, human integrity and dignity, truthfulness, private property) and warn us that we cannot do more harm than necessary in trying to achieve these values.[64]

5. *Richard A. McCormick.* Richard McCormick's annual "Moral Notes" in *Theological Studies* which reviews moral literature and comments on recent developments in moral theology have won him the esteem of moralists of every stripe. Since his opinions are so highly valued, his contribution to the discussion of the meaning and limits of material norms should not go unnoticed.

Like Knauer, Schüller, Fuchs, and Janssens, McCormick says that "proportionate reason" is decisive for determining right and wrong moral actions. McCormick's position, in summary, is that actions which cause non-moral evil (Knauer's "physical evil," Fuchs' "premoral evil," and Janssens' "ontic evil" or "premoral disvalue") are moral only if there is a truly proportionate reason which justifies the action. For example, taking life is wrong unless there is a proportionate reason to do so.

McCormick's greatest contribution to the discussion of norms is that he has borrowed selectively from Knauer, Schüller, Fuchs, Janssens, and others to flesh out in greater detail what constitutes a proportionate reason. McCormick, like his revisionist colleagues, does not maintain that any reason at all is a proportionate reason. Rather, he recognizes not only the decisiveness of the judgment of proportionality but also how difficult this judgment is to make. He wisely entitled the lecture in which he most thoroughly presented the criteria for a proportionate reason as *Ambiguity in Moral Choice.*[65] In this lecture he says:

Proportionate reason means three things: (a) a value at least equal to that sacrificed is at stake; (b) there is no less harmful way of protecting the values here and now; (c) the manner of its protection here and now will not undermine it in the long run.[66]

Put negatively, these criteria read as follows:

> An action is disproportionate in any of the following instances: if a lesser value is preferred to a more important one; if evil is unnecessarily caused in the protection of a greater good; if, in the circumstances, the manner of protecting the good will undermine it in the long run.[67]

McCormick has recently revised the third criterion in response to criticisms of his first effort. In a recent work, *Doing Evil To Achieve Good,* which he edited with Paul Ramsey, McCormick revises his third criterion by dropping the condition "in the long run." He explains his revision this way:

> Wrongfulness must be attributed to a lack of proportion. By that I mean that the value I am pursuing is being pursued in a way calculated in human judgment (not without prediscursive elements) to undermine it. I would further explain (tentatively) the disproportion in terms of an association of basic goods whereby the manner of protecting or pursuing a good brings other values or goods into play and can be responsible for disproportion as a result. In other words, I would abandon the *long-term effects* explanation of teleology; but I see no reason for abandoning the teleology itself.[68]

The judgment of the proper proportionality in the circumstances depends a great deal on how we define "in the circumstances." McCormick has given some guidelines on how to define this. He does not want to define the circumstances too narrowly. Nor does he want to define them in terms of the quantitative good that can be saved in a conflict of values. McCormick's guidelines for defining "in the circumstances" include the following: (1) Weigh the social implications and after-effects of an action insofar as they can be foreseen. (2) Use the test of generalizability: What if everyone in similar circumstances did this? (3) Consider the cultural climate with its tendencies to favor certain biases. (4) Draw upon the wisdom of past experiences especially as this wisdom is embodied in norms that have served humankind well through conflicts in the past. (5) Consult broadly, seeking the experience and reflection of others in order to prevent the strong influence of self-interest from biasing perception and judgment. (6) Allow the full force of one's religious beliefs to be brought to bear on interpreting the meaning of the moral conflict and to enlighten options.[69] This is the kind of homework McCormick requires if we are to assess proportionate reason properly.

In light of this understanding of proportionate reason, we can understand McCormick's interpretation of material norms. These norms are constant reminders of values and disvalues. They do not let us forget that when we are faced with a non-moral evil, or a disvalue, we cannot simply settle for it as though it were a good. To say that something is a non-moral evil or a disvalue, like war, contraception, or sterilization, is to imply that we ought to strive to the point where causing or permitting such a disvalue is no longer required. This means that material norms point out the kind of conduct that ought to be avoided as far as possible. However, in the world of inevitable conflict of values, causing or permitting non-moral evil to happen may be permitted with a proportionate reason. It is precisely this lack of proportionate reason that makes acting contrary to a concrete material norm, or causing non-moral evil, morally wrong.[70]

What McCormick demands for a proper consideration of proportionality requires the moral person to be very much reliant on communal discernment. Weighing of values in conflict is not and should not be an individualistic soul-searching. "Deciding by myself" has no place in assessing proportionality for McCormick. The meaning and limits of moral norms for McCormick direct the moral person to more moral consultation and guidance than would ever be called for when the norms were interpreted to propose certain actions as intrinsically evil in themselves and never justified.

This ends our report of a representative sampling of revisionist literature on moral norms. This survey shows that for the revisionist theologians there can be exceptions to material norms when there is a proportionate reason. To say that there can be exceptions to material norms is really nothing new in Catholic thought. St. Thomas said as much. In his treatment of natural law (*ST.* I-II, q. 94) he distinguishes universal principles (formal norms) which are absolute from secondary or concrete precepts (material norms) which are not always applicable (*valent ut in pluribus, ST.* I-II, q. 94, a. 4). His treatment of prudence (*ST.* II-II, q. 51, a. 4) affirms the same thing when he emphasizes that the consideration that makes up this virtue requires us to examine each situation in light of higher principles and not only material norms.

To admit to exceptions in material norms is not to deny their validity or usefulness. These norms continue to be useful to light up important premoral values and disvalues and to warn us that we ought not to cause more harm than we need to in order to do the good. Josef Fuchs, Louis Janssens, and Richard McCormick[71] argue that, *theoretically* speaking, we cannot claim concrete material norms as exceptionless. However, we ought *practically* to hold some as such. They call these kinds of material norms "practical absolutes" or "virtually exceptionless" moral norms. We need to take a brief look at what these are like.

Virtually Exceptionless Material Norms

The revisionist theologians make their theoretical and practical distinctions about the absoluteness of material norms on the basis that human actions are a mixture of premoral value and disvalue. There is probably no human action which does not have some mixture of good and bad. The moral choice in a love ethics ought to maximize premoral value and minimize premoral disvalue. So, to have an absolute material norm, we would have to be able to describe a physical action, apart from intention and circumstances, which causes so much premoral disvalue as to outweigh any conceivable good. To make such a claim for a physical action demands a foreknowledge of this action in all possible combinations of intentions and circumstances. The revisionist theologians claim that the limitations of human knowledge make such a vantage point theoretically impossible.[72]

However, the revisionist theologians maintain that some material norms are practical absolutes, or virtually exceptionless. This means that while it is theoretically impossible to demonstrate them as absolute, these norms highlight values which, in the general course of events, will take precedence and, for all practical purposes, should be preferred. Some examples are in order. Josef Fuchs, as we have seen, cannot conceive of any kind of exception to the norm which would prohibit "cruel treatment of a child which is of no benefit to the child."[73] Richard McCormick speaks of "the direct killing of non-combatants in warfare"[74] as a practical absolute. Louis Janssens identifies "You shall render help to a person in extreme distress" and the prohibition of rape as two examples of virtually exceptionless norms.[75] Paul Ramsey includes rape along with "Never experiment medically on a human being without his informed consent," "Never punish a man whom one knows to be innocent of that for which he would be punished," and "No premarital intercourse" as being significantly closed to exceptions.[76] Thomas L. Beauchamp and James F. Childress place in the same category this norm, "Always obtain the informed consent of your competent patients except in emergency or low-risk situations."[77] As with Fuchs' "cruel treatment" and Ramsey's "pre-marital" (which for him is not the same as pre-ceremonial), there might be considerable debate about what constitues an "emergency" or "low-risk" in the Beauchamp-Childress example.[78] Nevertheless, what these examples show is that some material norms can and should be regarded as virtually exceptionless.

What is the force of saying "virtually" exceptionless? For McCormick, "virtually" indicates that we cannot prove with the sharpness of a syllogistic click that no exception could ever occur. The conclusion that we ought to hold some material norms as "virtually" exceptionless is based on a prudential judgment that weighs the values at stake in light of past experience of human failure, inconsistency, and frailty, and in light of a certain agnosticism with regard to long-term effects. These norms light up values which, in the general course of events and for all practical purposes, ought to take precedence even though their preference in every instance cannot be absolutely demonstrated.[79]

For Donald Evans, who coined the expression "virtually exceptionless," the point of saying "virtually" is to avoid a "creeping legalism" which tries to extend the range of moral absolutes farther than can be justified. Evans sees moral norms on a continuum. Some are open to extensive revision, some less open, and others are in varying degrees virtually exceptionless. "Virtually" respects the freedom and discretion of the moral agent, the ambiguity of moral action, the limitation of human knowing, and the limitations of any attempt to capture the experience of value in a pithy formula. The force of being "virtually" exceptionless also puts the burden of proof on those who would want to make an exception.[80]

For Albert DiIanni, the force of being "virtually" exceptionless means that while we cannot theoretically demonstrate their absoluteness, we ought to teach these norms and act *as if* they were absolute. To be virtually exceptionless for DiIanni means that there are no live options to these norms. Since their practical exceptions are so unimaginable, we ought to live with them and regard them in our moral education as being absolute.[81]

Conclusion: The Strategy of Mixed Consequentialism

The place that moral norms are given in the mixed consequentialism of the revisionist theologians can be seen more clearly when we consider the strategy of decision-making of this approach. I have diagramed this strategy in Figure 3. This strategy gives significant attention to consequences, but *not only* to consequences. It also gives due attention to moral norms, but the norms are not ultimately determinative of the moral decision.

The strategy of mixed consequentialism is somewhat complex and very demanding. It must try to account for the complexity of moral reality as much as possible. This means that it must consider the uniqueness of the moral agent and the moral dilemma, the continuity of the present moral experience with similar ones of the past and so allow for an appeal to moral norms, and that it must weigh the values in conflict. This strategy tries to discover which options deserve preference in light of all the values at stake; it tries to determine the means truly proportionate to the good intended and the evil inevitably caused without ever losing a grasp on the basic goods that define the human possibility for growth. This strategy tries to avoid the common error of reducing moral choice to only two alternatives

Figure 3
MIXED CONSEQUENTIALISM

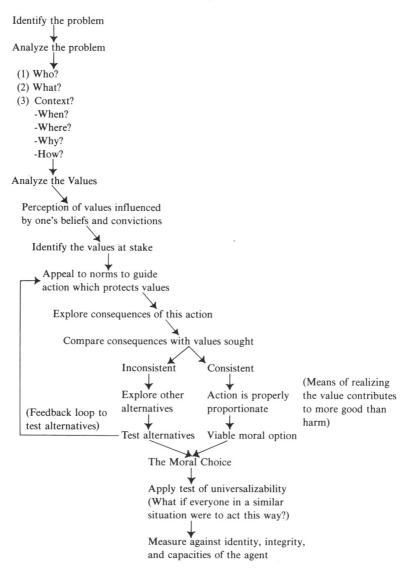

Identify the problem

Analyze the problem

(1) Who?
(2) What?
(3) Context?
   -When?
   -Where?
   -Why?
   -How?

Analyze the Values

Perception of values influenced
by one's beliefs and convictions

Identify the values at stake

Appeal to norms to guide
action which protects values

Explore consequences of this action

Compare consequences with values sought

Inconsistent   Consistent

                                              (Means of realizing
Explore other   Action is properly   the value contributes
alternatives   proportionate   to more good than
                                              harm)
(Feedback loop to
test alternatives)

Test alternatives   Viable moral option

The Moral Choice

Apply test of universalizability
(What if everyone in a similar
situation were to act this way?)

Measure against identity, integrity,
and capacities of the agent

(an "either-or" forced choice) and then weighing one against the other, or of considering only the immediate and not the long-range consequences.

Since it is impossible to have in view all possible alternatives and consequences, the moral decision of mixed consequentialism is made with some degree of uncertainty. The goal of moral analysis is to reduce this uncertainty to manageable size, and to insure that due consideration has been given to at least the most obvious alternatives and outstanding consequences, both of which can be determined on the basis of past personal and communal experiences and by means of scientific methods.

What is decisive in the deliberations of mixed consequentialism is the judgment whether a proportion exists between premoral evil (disvalue) that inevitably occurs in any human action and the good (value) the person seeks by acting. The action is finally chosen on the basis that the good (value) intended outweighs the evil (disvalue) that is produced. The heart of the moral choice lies in the judgment about the proportion and the good that the action achieves. If there is no value proportionate to the disvalue produced, then the action is morally evil. But not until this judgment of proportion is made can the action be considered a moral one at all.

The Deontologist Position

This third kind of approach to moral norms and the moral rightness or wrongness of actions is represented on the Catholic side by Germain Grisez and William E. May, and on the Protestant side by Paul Ramsey. While there are some areas of difference between these theologians, they share a common deontological orientation. The deontological orientation denies that the morally good is determined solely by consequences (the strict consequentialist or "situationist" view). A deontological approach will hold that there are at least some acts, or categories of acts, which are right or wrong no matter what the consequences, e.g., keeping promises is always right, killing the innocent is always wrong. In the deontological approach the norm becomes the principal reference by which actions are judged to be morally right or wrong.

1. *Germain Grisez and William E. May.* On the Catholic side,

Germain Grisez has been an articulate spokesman for this position. Since William E. May shares so much in common with Grisez, a summary of Grisez' position will suffice to represent this position.[82] Grisez' approach rides on the key notion of basic human goods. He identifies eight basic human goods: life, activities engaged in for their own sake, experiences sought for their own sake, knowledge pursued for its own sake, integrity, genuineness, justice and friendship, worship and holiness.[83] These basic human goods are possible purposes for moral action and the source for deriving principles for practical reason. "The practical principles thus express not what *is* so, but what-is-to-be through our own action."[84] For example, from the basic good of life we can derive the principle of self-preservation. "Life is a good whose requirements are to be served; actions which promote it should be done; what is opposed to it should be avoided."[85]

The basic human goods, as principles of practical reason, clarify what is possible in moral choice but do not determine by themselves why some choices are morally good and others are morally evil. What determines this? For Grisez, moral goodness and evil depend on the attitude of the moral person. A right attitude makes good choices. What is a right attitude? Grisez answers:

It is realistic, in the sense that it conforms fully with reality. To choose a particular good with an appreciation of its genuine but limited possibility and its objectively human character is to choose it with an attitude of realism. Such choice does not attempt to transform and belittle the goodness of what is not chosen, but only to realize what is chosen.

The attitude which leads to immoral choices, by contrast, narrows the good to the possibilities one chooses to realize. The good is not appreciated in its objectively human character, simply as a good, but as *this* good of *such* a sort to be achieved *by me*. Instead of conforming to the real amplitude of human possibility, such an attitude transforms that possibility by restriction. Immoral choice forecloses possibilities merely because they are not chosen; rather than merely realizing some goods while leaving others unrealized, such choice presumes to negate what it does not embrace in order to exalt what it chooses. Goods equally ultimate are reduced to the status of mere means for maximizing preferred possibilities; principles of practical reason as fundamental as those that make the choice possible are brushed aside as if they wholly lacked validity.[86]

These sentences capture the heart of Grisez' approach. The implication of this position is that a moral choice must be made with an attitude of openness to all goods, even those not chosen. Each basic good must be allowed to exercise its influence. All basic goods hold a primary place in moral reasoning. Since the basic human goods are equally basic, one good cannot be subordinated to another. (This is what Fletcher's strict consequentialism does when it seeks the greatest good for the greatest number.) To choose directly an action which inhibits the realization of one of the basic goods in order to maximize another is to restrict what is simply good to what is good according to one particular choice. "But we should be more interested in *the good* than in *our* good,"[87] maintains Grisez.

On the basis of the right moral attitude open to all goods, Grisez derives the norm that human life, a basic good, must be respected. However, even this norm is not without exception for him. He says:

Not even the parent and physician need always act to preserve and promote life, for sometimes other goods also are very pressing. A proper moral attitude is compatible with the omission of action that would realize a good, provided that omission itself is essential to realize another good (or the same generic good in another instance).[88]

However, what is binding with greater strictness is acting *directly* against a basic good or acting in a way that *directly* interferes with realizing a basic good. For Grisez, it is one thing to allow the destruction or interference of a basic good to occur as an unavoidable side-effect of an effort to pursue a basic good. But it is quite another thing to act directly against or to interfere directly with realizing a basic good. On this basis, Grisez maintains that it is never permitted to take human life *directly.*[89] Likewise, Grisez claims that contraception is intrinsically immoral on the grounds that it is an act which presupposes an intention directly opposed to the procreative good, which is a basic requirement for initiating life.[90] Since Grisez begins with the presupposition that there are certain basic human goods against which one may never directly act, he holds to the absolute prohibition of masturbation, contraception, direct sterilization, artificial insemination, abortion, homosexuality, and extra-marital sex. Since these are actions which turn against a basic good, they are morally evil.

William E. May summarizes the essence of the deontological approach like that taken by Grisez in a way that will serve as a fitting conclusion:

> . . . a human being cannot rightfully do a deed that is destructive of a human good such as life, unless in the doing of that deed the agent's intent and the thrust of his act are both targeted on the good achievable in and through that deed. In such instances the evil caused is an inevitable and inescapable element or partial aspect of the entire human deed, and the evil is an aspect that is not of necessity intended by the doer. Such deeds may be directly destructive of a human good in a *physical* way, but they are not directly destructive in the order of human intentionality inasmuch as they are not intended in any proper sense but are rather foreseen and permitted. . . . I ought not to be willing to do a deed that will require, as an inevitable necessity, that I am willing to set myself in my will (biblically my "heart") against a real good of another human being, of another being of moral worth, that requires me to say of these goods here and now that they are non-goods, no longer worthy of my love and respect.[91]

One of the key points of difference between Grisez and May and the revisionist theologians lies in their understanding of the kind of evil that is at stake in turning against a basic good. For Grisez and May directly turning against basic goods is a *moral* evil. For the revisionists this could only be classified in itself as an *ontic* or *premoral* evil.

2. *Paul Ramsey*. From very early in Ramsey's career, "obedient love" has dominated his exposition of Christian ethics. "Obedient love" is very closely associated with the idea of "covenant" for him, which has been a principal deontological notion throughout his career. In his early major work, *Basic Christian Ethics,* Ramsey says:

> The covenant means unconditional obedience; it means unclaiming love. In this book, the basic norm for Christian ethics has been called "obedient love" because of its intimate association with the idea of "covenant" and with the "reign" of God.[92]

For Ramsey, covenants have authority and are obligatory as they define basic duties which make claims binding on the persons in the covenant relationship. The existence of covenants with their canons of loyalty and claims of fidelity give rise to norms that identify those kinds of actions which are right and wrong and assure continuity and stability in the moral life.[93]

Norms emerge from covenant relationships and serve persons by putting forward the constants that promote the true human good. These norms are Ramsey's "love-formed principles of conduct."[94] Person-centered norms derived from covenant claims of loyalty and fidelity should have priority over consequences. For Ramsey, persons are likely to suffer more rather than less if moral judgments are determined by immediate consequences rather than by moral norms. Norms provide consistency and stability to the moral life. The degree to which the norms are regarded as exceptionless hinges to a great extent on the different understandings of the relevant moral terms used in the norms, such as lying, murder, stealing, adultery, etc.[95] The exceptionless character that Ramsey attributes to norms manifests his concern over creeping exceptionism in the moral life and his desire to preserve continuity and stability in the moral life of persons and society.

Conclusion: The Strategy of Deontologism

The strategy for decision-making of deontologism helps us appreciate the significance this approach gives to moral norms. I have

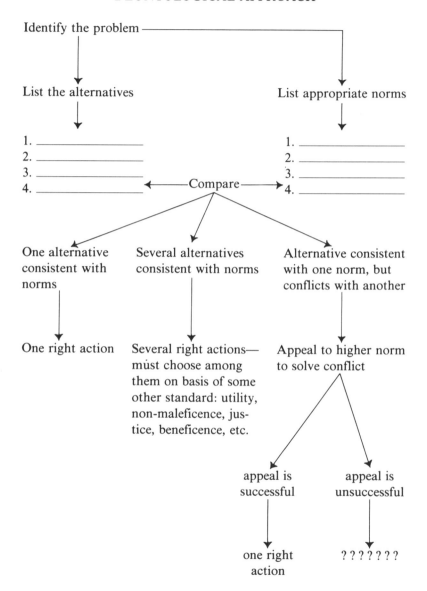

Figure 4
DEONTOLOGICAL APPROACH

Identify the problem

List the alternatives

List appropriate norms

1. _____
2. _____
3. _____
4. _____

Compare

1. _____
2. _____
3. _____
4. _____

One alternative consistent with norms

Several alternatives consistent with norms

Alternative consistent with one norm, but conflicts with another

One right action

Several right actions—must choose among them on basis of some other standard: utility, non-maleficence, justice, beneficence, etc.

Appeal to higher norm to solve conflict

appeal is successful

appeal is unsuccessful

one right action

? ? ? ? ? ? ?

diagramed this strategy in Figure 4.[96] The deontological approach holds that the standard of right and wrong consists in one or more rules, or norms. These norms are valid and applicable whether they promote the greatest good or not. Judgments about what to do in a particular case are to be made on the basis of the norm.

The deontologist holds that some acts, or categories of acts, are right or wrong no matter what the consequences, e.g., telling the truth and keeping promises are always right, killing the innocent is always wrong. In short, the deontological position maintains that there are some acts which are always and everywhere "intrinsically morally evil." When these acts are the major moral term in the formulation of the moral norm, then the norm becomes the standard point of reference for judging the morality of an act.

The strategy of decision-making for the deontologist will give a significant place to norms. Alternative courses of action must correspond to an appropriate norm. If the alternative is in accord with a norm, then the action is morally right. If several alternatives are in accordance with appropriate norms, then several possible moral actions are available and the moral person must choose among them. The choice among alternatives is made according to some other criteria. If an alternative is in accordance with one norm (such as "Always keep promises") but would conflict with another (such as "Give back what belongs to another"), then appeal has to be made to a higher level norm (such as "Protect life"). The deontologist cannot modify norms since they have validity independently of consequences. In situations where norms conflict, rearranging priorities is the only way out of the dilemma.

Conclusion

From this review of the literature, we can see that there is no monolithic theory of morality today that supports only one approach to moral reasoning or to the meaning and limits of moral norms. Consequently, we do not have universally accepted sets of moral solutions common to all moralists.

The developments in Catholic moral theology have taken place in dialogue with Protestant ethics. The strict consequentialism of Jo-

seph Fletcher, however, has not found a following among the leading
Catholic moralists. Although this approach has been a provocative
critique of traditional Catholic morality, and many of the developments in Catholic morality have occurred in response to it, the deontological orientation has kept Catholic morality close to its tradition
in many ways. This approach shares an attitude toward norms and
many moral solutions that is similar to the traditional Catholic approach. The revisionist approach of contemporary morality has
broken through the weakness of traditional Catholic morality which
was rather tight and closed in its method and substance. The developing revisionist critique reflects, for the most part, an openness not
found in traditional Catholic moral theology, nor in recent deontological approaches. The revisionist approach has the advantage of addressing a wide range of complex and morally problematic human
situations with a respect for the personal and social factors that make
a moral judgment difficult but closer to human experience. The revisionist critique has opened conversation with other disciplines, especially the empirical sciences, in order to pose new ways of understanding the moral person and moral actions, and of evaluating consequences of actions and policies. But these advantages do not come
without a price. With the revisionist approach being free of the re-
strictions which once offered clear and universally applicable moral
norms and decisions, we no longer have universally accepted sets of
conclusions common to all Catholic moralists.

Catholic and Protestant moral theology share in common a serious concern that surfaces at the level of practical moral reasoning.
James M. Gustafson expressed it well when he said:

> . . . how can the Christian community and its members
> make moral decisions and moral judgments which are both
> responsive and responsible: responsive to problems emerg-
> ing in contemporary science and technology, political and
> social institutions, and interpersonal life; responsible not
> only for the consequences of actions in new circumstances,
> but responsible also to the moral values, the moral princi-
> ples, that are grounded in the faith and life of the Christian
> community, and to the moral values and principles that are
> grounded in our common humanity.[97]

This is the great challenge that faces the future development of moral theology.

With this marked pluralism in contemporary moral theology, and the never-ending challenge to make moral decisions and judgments that are both responsive and responsible, how does one proceed with meeting the responsibilities of pastoral guidance in moral matters? This is the issue of the next and last chapter. Since the revisionist approach to moral norms and practical moral reasoning has attracted so much attention in recent years, we will focus on this approach in pastoral guidance.

Notes

1. *The Moral Choice,* p. 220.

2. "Norms and Priorities in a Love Ethics," *Louvain Studies* 4 (Spring 1977): 207.

3. "The Question of Moral Norms," *American Ecclesiastical Review* 169 (June 1975): 385–386.

4. O'Connell, *Principles for a Catholic Morality,* pp. 160–162.

5. O'Connell, "The Question of Moral Norms," p. 386.

6. "Norms and Priorities in a Love Ethics," p. 208.

7. *Ibid.,* p. 216.

8. Traditionally, these kinds of actions are considered *secundum se* evils. This means that these actions carried their own absolute condemnation in their very name (*mox nominata sunt mala*). The very meaning of the name joins the material action to a sinful intention (*ex libidine*). The essence of *secundum se* evil actions is to be immoral so that such an action can never be made good by any configuration of intention and circumstances. John Dedek has provided two valuable historical studies which explore this sense of moral absolutes in St. Thomas and his predecessors. The first study was "Moral Absolutes in the Predecessors of St. Thomas," *Theological Studies* 38 (December 1977): 654–680. The second was "Intrinsically Evil Acts: An Historical Study of the Mind of St. Thomas," *The Thomist* 43 (July 1979): 385–413. For another historical essay with similar findings, see Franz Scholz, "Problems on Norms Raised by Ethical Borderline Situations: Beginnings of a Solution in Thomas Aquinas and Bonaventure," in *Readings in Moral Theology No. 1,* pp. 158–183.

9. Richard A. McCormick has explained these issues regarding synthetic terms well in his "Moral Notes," *Theological Studies* 37 (March 1976): 73–74; 39 (March 1978): 93.

10. O'Connell, "The Question of Moral Norms," pp. 385–387; also *Principles for a Catholic Morality*, pp. 161–162. Louis Janssens, "Norms and Priorities in a Love Ethics," p. 209.

11. *Principles for a Catholic Morality*, pp. 161–162.

12. For Curran's analysis, see "Utilitarianism and Contemporary Moral Theology: Situating the Debates," *Themes*, p. 133; also in *Readings in Moral Theology No. 1*, p. 352. For McCormick's analysis, see "Reflections on the Literature," in *Readings in Moral Theology No. 1*, p. 318; also in "Moral Notes," *Theological Studies* 38 (March 1977): 82.

13. *Situation Ethics: The New Morality* (Philadelphia: Westminster Press, 1966).

14. *Ibid.*, pp. 18–31.

15. *Ibid.*, p. 95.

16. *Ibid.*, p. 26.

17. *Ibid.*, p. 30.

18. This figure follows closely the one drawn by Howard Brody in *Ethical Decisions in Medicine* (Boston: Little, Brown and Co., 1976), p. A-2b.

19. "The Hermeneutic Function of the Principle of Double Effect," *Natural Law Forum* 12 (1967): 132–162. I am following this version as it has been reproduced in *Readings in Moral Theology No. 1*, pp. 1–39.

20. *Ibid.*, p. 10.

21. *Ibid.*, p. 21.

22. *Ibid.*, p. 2.

23. *Ibid.*

24. *Ibid.*, pp. 6, 27.

25. *Ibid.*, pp. 10–14, 27.

26. *Ibid.*, pp. 6, 14, 26.

27. *Ibid.*, pp. 32–33.

28. *Ibid.*, p. 22.

29. *Ibid.*, p. 26.

30. *Ibid.*, pp. 31–34.

31. "Zur Problematik allgemein verbindlicher ethischer Grundsätze," *Theologie und Philosophie* 45 (1970): 4. I have accepted this translation found in "What Ethical Principles Are Universally Valid?" *Theology Digest* 19 (March 1971): 24. I will use the *Digest* version for this summary review.

32. "Moral Notes," *Theological Studies* 32 (March 1971): 90.

33. "Various Types of Grounding for Ethical Norms," in *Readings in Moral Theology No. 1*, p. 190.

34. Schüller, "What Ethical Principles Are Universally Valid?" p. 25.

35. *Ibid.*, pp. 26–27.

36. Josef Fuchs—"The Absoluteness of Moral Terms," *Gregorianum* 52

(1971): 415–457. I will follow the reproduced version in *Readings in Moral Theology No. 1*, pp. 94–137.

37. *Ibid.*, p. 119.

38. *Ibid.*

39. *Ibid.*, p. 120.

40. *Ibid.*, p. 124.

41. *Ibid.*, p. 121.

42. *Ibid.*

43. *Ibid.*, p. 125.

44. *Ibid.*, p. 126.

45. *Ibid.*

46. *Louvain Studies* 4 (Fall 1972): 115–156. I will follow the reprinted version in *Readings in Moral Theology No. 1*, pp. 40–93.

47. *Ibid.*, p. 44.

48. *Ibid.*, p. 49.

49. *Ibid.*

50. *Ibid.*, p. 51.

51. *Ibid.*, p. 52.

52. *Ibid.*, p. 55.

53. *Ibid.*, pp. 56–58.

54. "Norms and Priorities in a Love Ethics," *Louvain Studies* 4 (Spring 1977): 207–238. Throughout this article, Janssens uses "premoral disvalue" in the same sense that he uses "ontic evil" in his earlier article, "Ontic Evil and Moral Evil."

55. "Ontic Evil and Moral Evil," in *Readings in Moral Theology No. 1*, p. 60.

56. *Ibid.*, p. 61.

57. *Ibid.*, pp. 67–68.

58. *Ibid.*, p. 71.

59. *Ibid.*, pp. 72–73.

60. *Ibid.*, p. 78.

61. *Ibid.*, p. 80.

62. "Norms and Priorities in a Love Ethics," pp. 213–214.

63. "Ontic Evil and Moral Evil," *Readings in Moral Theology No. 1*, p. 216.

64. *Ibid.*, p. 86. Also, "Norms and Priorities in a Love Ethics," p. 216.

65. Pere Marquette Lecture of 1973 at Marquette University (Milwaukee: Marquette University Press, 1973). This is reprinted as the first chapter in *Doing Evil To Achieve Good*, edited by Richard A. McCormick and Paul Ramsey (Chicago: Loyola University Press, 1978), pp. 7–53.

66. In the Marquette University edition, p. 93; in *Doing Evil*, p. 45.

67. In the Marquette University edition, p. 94; in *Doing Evil,* p. 45.

68. "A Commentary on the Commentaries," in *Doing Evil,* p. 265.

69. In the Marquette University edition, pp. 95–96; in *Doing Evil,* p. 46.

70. "Moral Norms and Their Meaning," *Lectureship,* edited by Mount Angel Abbey (St. Benedict, Oregon: Mount Angel Abbey, 1978), pp. 43–46.

71. For Fuchs, see "Absoluteness of Moral Terms," in *Readings in Moral Theology No. 1,* pp. 125–126; for Janssens, see "Norms and Priorities in a Love Ethics," pp. 217–218; for McCormick, see *Ambiguity in Moral Choice,* in the Marquette University edition, pp. 86, 87, 92; in *Doing Evil,* pp. 42–44.

72. See Chapter Two above, the section "The Knowledge of Realty," for the theoretical support to this claim of the limitations of human knowing.

73. "Absoluteness of Moral Terms," in *Readings in Moral Theology No. 1,* p. 126.

74. *Ambiguity in Moral Choice,* in Marquette University edition, pp. 86–93; in *Doing Evil,* pp. 42–44.

75. "Norms and Priorities in a Love Ethics," p. 217. However, just how Janssens sees the norm prohibiting rape to differ from a synthetic, formal norm is not readily evident.

76. "The Case of the Curious Exception," *Norm and Context in Christian Ethics,* edited by Outka and Ramsey, pp. 67–135.

77. *Principles of Biomedical Ethics* (New York: Oxford University Press, 1979), p. 43.

78. Donald Evans has made a good analysis of the significance of words with "elastic" meanings in norms such as these. See his study of Paul Ramsey in "Paul Ramsey on Exceptionless Moral Rules," *The American Journal of Jurisprudence* 16 (1971): 184–214, esp. 198 ff.

79. McCormick, *Ambiguity in Moral Choice* in the Marquette University edition, pp. 86–93; in *Doing Evil,* pp. 42–44.

80. Evans, "Paul Ramsey on Exceptionless Moral Rules," pp. 205–207. See also his article, "Love, Situations, and Rules," *Norm and Context in Christian Ethics,* pp. 367–414, esp. pp. 402–414.

81. DiIanni, "The Direct/Indirect Distinction in Morals," in *Readings in Moral Theology No. 1,* pp. 215–243, esp. 236–238.

82. William E. May expresses and shows his affinity with the approach of Germain Grisez in *Becoming Human* (Dayton: Pflaum Publishing Co., 1975); see especially Chapter Four, pp. 79–112. Also, see May's "Ethics and Human Identity: The Challenge of the New Biology," *Horizons* 3 (Spring 1976): 17–37.

83. Germain Grisez, *Abortion: The Myths, the Realities, and the Arguments* (New York: Corpus Books, 1970), pp. 312–313.

84. *Ibid.,* p. 314.

85. Germain Grisez, *Contraception and Natural Law* (Milwaukee: Bruce Publishing Co., 1964), p. 65.

86. Grisez, *Abortion,* p. 315.

87. *Ibid.,* p. 318.

88. *Ibid.,* p. 319.

89. *Ibid.,* pp. 319–320.

90. Grisez, *Contraception and Natural Law;* see especially the chapter, "Why Contraception Is Immoral," pp. 76–106.

91. "Ethics and Human Identity: The Challenge of the New Biology," *Horizons* 3 (Spring 1976): 36–37. May reflects a strict deontological position in his "Sterilization: Catholic Teaching and Catholic Practice," *Homiletic and Pastoral Review* 87 (August–September, 1977): 9–23.

92. *Basic Christian Ethics* (New York: Charles Scribner's Sons, 1950), p. 388. This major work is now available in Midway Reprint (Chicago: University of Chicago Press, 1978).

93. Paul Ramsey, "The Case of the Curious Exception," *Norm and Context in Christian Ethics,* pp. 126–127. See also, "The Biblical Norm of Righteousness," *Interpretation* 24 (October 1970): 419–429.

94. Paul Ramsey, *Deeds and Rules in Christian Ethics* (New York: Charles Scribner's Sons, 1967), pp. 126–133 at 132.

95. Ramsey, "The Case of the Curious Exception, pp. 74–93.

96. Figure 4 follows closely the one drawn by Howard Brody in *Ethical Decisions in Medicine,* p. A-2a.

97. *Protestant and Roman Catholic Ethics* (Chicago: University of Chicago Press, 1978), p. 33.

5
Moral Norms and Pastoral Guidance

At this point, many who bear the pastoral responsibility of giving moral guidance may be wondering about the possible implications of this contemporary discussion of moral norms. There is not room here to pursue the implications of the three major approaches to moral norms. Since so much attention has been given to the revisionist approach to moral norms and moral reasoning in recent years, we will explore pastoral implications of that approach. But first, we may be well served by identifying some of the major points of criticism directed against the revisionist approach. Then we will consider the pastoral implications which the revisionists are making of their approach.

Revisionist Theology and Its Critics

The revisionist approach has received a fair amount of criticism from those favoring a deontological approach to moral norms and moral reasoning. The most vocal critics have been John Connery, Germain Grisez, William E. May, Paul M. Quay, and Paul Ramsey.[1] Here we can only identify briefly three chief difficulties which the critics point out.

1. *The revisionist approach is subject to ethical relativism.* One difficulty the critics point to in the revisionist approach is that it leaves its formulations of moral norms and its judgments of propor-

tionality in moral reasoning subject to historically situated and conditioned moral communities. The critics say that the revisionist approach does not provide grounds for transcending one's personal, communal, or cultural situation in order to provide a transcultural, transhistorical, universal standard.

William E. May is one who sees this kind of relativism as a major problem, " . . . insofar as it locates the right-making or wrong-making factor in the judgment of the community, not in the nature of the act or practice."[2] May is supported on this score by Benedict M. Ashley and Kevin D. O'Rourke. For them the Gospel provides the transcultural, transhistorical standard against which to judge and reformulate moral norms. The Gospel confirms and surpasses the order of creation, or natural law. O'Rourke and Ashley do not want to reduce natural law to human reason alone to account for all factors of a moral situation:

> For Aquinas to say that natural law is human reason includes the affirmation that our human reason rightly used can discover a purposeful order in the world prior to any willed human purpose. Our willed human purposes must conform to this natural order if they are to be fully human and ethical. We can discover these natural purposes in the innate needs of our human persons, in their common biological and psychological structures, and in the fundamental social relations upon which the survival of our human community depends.[3]

For this reason the revision of moral norms in light of the Gospel and natural law must rest on the absolute character of innate human needs and fundamental social relations. Thus there will always be some kinds of human acts which are intrinsically morally evil, that is, some kinds of human acts which are violations of the rights and obligations innate to persons and societies and which have no exception.

The issues at stake in this point of criticism are many. At least three are the meaning of being historically conditioned, the epistemological presuppositions and procedures which would enable one to grasp clearly the founding rights and obligations innate in human persons and societies, and the complex problems that are part of moral discernment, individual and communal.

2. *The revisionist approach is a form of extrinsic ethics.* Following closely upon the criticism of ethical relativism is the criticism of extrinsicism. "Extrinsicism" in ethics is the claim that moral significance is given to action by something outside the action, namely the intention of the agent and/or the consequences. The point of this criticism is that the revisionist approach is an arbitrary way of determining the morality of concrete acts. This is because the revisionists do not hold to any absolute material norms, and assert that no action considered apart from circumstances and intention can be judged "intrinsically morally evil." Without an "intrinsic" morality there is no sure basis upon which to measure the relative importance of values.

John Connery is a critic who has identified this difficulty with the revisionist approach. He interprets the revisionist approach as "a moral system that makes the judgment of an act depend solely on its consequences."[4] For Connery, the basic problem with a morality based solely on consequences is not only that its norms remain open to exceptions, but that this approach "allows exceptions which go against commonly held convictions."[5] Ashley and O'Rourke find the basic problem to be this: "Once we abandon intrinsic morality and make the principle of proportion the primary determinant, it is no longer clear how such an evaluation [of relative importance of value and disvalue] can be made."[6]

William E. May objects to the revisionist claim that an action described in non-moral terms cannot be considered intrinsically morally evil. For May there are some kinds of acts, described in non-moral terms, that simply cannot be freely chosen if the person wishes to act morally. In short, he maintains that there are some kinds of human acts which are intrinsically morally evil in themselves and which no intention, circumstances, or consequences could ever purify. Concrete material norms expressing these kinds of actions are universally true and without exception. May gives the following as examples of such norms:

> It is always wrong to have coition with a brute animal; it is always wrong to intend directly the torture of another hu-

man being; it is always wrong to use public monies to pay one's mistress.[7]

The issue at stake in this second area of difficulty centers on the proper identification of the human act. What constitutes the moral significance of the human act? How does one really describe what is being done?

3. *The revisionist approach tries to measure the unmeasurable.* The third area of difficulty often cited about revisionist theology is that it is a system that depends on a quantitative summary of values. Determining the moral good becomes merely a quantitative process where values are traded off for one anotber. The difficulty with such an approach is that it leads to a disregard for the uniqueness and diverse kinds of values at stake in a moral dilemma. Without recognizing the qualitative difference of values, the revisionist approach too easily measures the unmeasurable. For example, how weigh and mcasurc thc valuc of thc lifc of a dcfcctive newborn against the cost of treatment, the burdens of the infant's parents and to society, and so on?

Paul M. Quay has challenged the measuring or "calculation" of values that he finds in the revisionist approach. The heart of Quay's criticism is that the revisionists, or, as he calls them, the "value" theologians do not properly distinguish good and value, or evil and disvalue.[8] For Quay, unlike the revisionists, positive values and good are not the same, and disvalues are not the same as premoral (ontic) evils. Quay claims that not all the elements needed for making a moral judgment can be reduced to values. Failing to distinguish good and value leads, in Quay's mind, to making what is morally good a negotiable thing. The result is that moral dilemmas are resolved by a quantitative process of trading off values. Quay makes this evaluation of the revisionist approach:

> Evcrything can in principle be evaluated and scaled in accord with utility, worth, and price; as values are balanced, exchanged, and traded off for one another, the moral judgment becomes a commerce and merchandising in human conduct and Christian behavior.[9]

Germain Grisez and Paul Ramsey share a similar criticism of the revisionist differences of values. Their criticism is summarized well in this statement of Grisez, "There is no 'greatest net good,' since goods are incomparable."[10] Their point is that since basic goods cannot be measured one against the other, the revisionist attempt to assess proportionality is endangered. Since basic goods are incommensurable, they conclude to the immorality of directly turning against a basic good.

The issue that this point of criticism raises is the need for a consistent theory of values which shows the source of values and the relationship between values, or basic goods, themselves and with the moral agent.

Moral theologians will continue to clarify their analyses and their language as the exchanges progress. In the meantime, the revisionist approach to moral norms and practical moral reasoning as it has been developed thus far has significant implications for pastoral guidance in moral matters. Some of these implications have surfaced in the literature of the revisionist theologians. The remainder of this chapter sketches briefly some of what has appeared in this literature.

Revisionist Theology and the Episcopal Magisterium

What status can we give to the method of moral reasoning and the interpretation of moral norms being developed by the revisionist moral theologians? What is the relation of revisionist theology to the episcopal magisterium? Do the opinions of the revisionist theologians, even when not sufficiently endorsed or influenced by official pronouncements of the episcopal magisterium, deserve a hearing? Do they have a rightful place in the formation of conscience? Questions like these are common to pastorally sensitive persons who must give moral guidance in the midst of the rich pluralism in Catholic morality today. Since the relation of the opinions of the revisionist theologians to the normative teaching of the episcopal moral magisterium is so crucial in pastoral moral guidance, we will begin with that.

Pius XII in his encyclical *Humani Generis* of 1950 acknowledged that whenever the Pope took an explicit stand on an issue, the issue was to be considered settled and no longer a matter for free debate among theologians and no alternative options to the position taken by the Pope were realistically available.[11] This would seem to put an end to the possibility of giving the opinions of the revisionist theologians a hearing.

Since the encyclical letter *Humanae Vitae* of Paul VI in 1968, however, there has been extensive study of the binding power of undefined, non-infallible teaching of the episcopal magisterium, especially in moral matters. The question of legitimate dissent from authoritative, non-infallible teaching has often been the subject of such studies.[12] These studies recognize that there are various grades and degrees of teaching authority in the Catholic Church. The formal distinctions of infallible teaching of the extraordinary magisterium and authentic, non-infallible teaching of the ordinary magisterium are the common way of making the distinction. There is general agreement that there have been no teachings on morality *defined* as infallible. This does not mean that the moral teachings we do have are meaningless, useless, or irrational. It means simply that these teachings are subject to re-evaluation and revision. The non-infallible teachings admit of different degrees in the way they are exercised. For example, an encyclical letter is more solemn than a papal address to a particular group. Whereas the response to infallible teaching is to be the assent of faith, the response to non-infallible teaching is to be a religious assent of mind and will (*LG,* n. 25). By virtue of the non-infallible character of the teaching of the ordinary magisterium, the response to it is conditional and the possibility of error and revision of the teaching exists.

By accepting the limitations that the episcopal moral magisterium has to face in regard to specific moral cases and in the formulation of material moral norms, we in no way diminish the normative character of the teaching authority of the episcopal magisterium nor the respect due it. Where specific moral cases and moral norms are concerned, the episcopal magisterium remains normative and functions within the pastoral domain by making judgments of prudence. As normative, these prudential judgments of an office that has the well-being of the human community at heart deserves the presumption of certainty on the part of the faithful.

There are good reasons why one should give official teaching of the Church on moral matters the presumption in its favor. One reason is that Catholics believe that the Holy Spirit dwells within the whole Church to guide and illumine its actions. Another reason is that the sources of moral wisdom (such as Scripture, the teaching of theologians past and present, scientific information, broad human experience, and the witness of moral lives, to name but a few) are so many and complex that it is hard for any one person to know about all of them, to understand them, or to put them together to make a good decision. Furthermore, the episcopal moral magisterium of the Church approaches moral issues with a concern to protect and improve human dignity. The episcopal magisterium can draw upon worldwide resources to overcome the biases of a particular culture when putting a moral perspective together and taking a moral stand. For reasons like these an attitude of openness of mind that desires to learn from this teaching and a readiness of will to assimilate the teaching and make it one's own is the proper and first response due the official teaching of the Church.[13] This kind of response gives the respect to normative teaching that is proportionate to the authority of the pastoral office of the episcopal magisterium.

At the same time, however, in accepting the many advantages that the episcopal magisterium has in taking a moral stand, and in giving the presumption of certainty in its favor, we cannot exclude all possible disagreement between the episcopal magisterium and the faithful. Nor does it seem that when such disagreement arises the magisterium will always be right and those who disagree will always be wrong. In the second chapter, we saw the importance of having everyone involved in the journey of coming to truth. Everyone contributes according to his or her own proper competence. Mutual sharing in the teaching-learning process involves ongoing dialogue between the magisterium and the faithful and the collaboration of various perspectives in order to come to a fuller grasp of truth and more adequate expressions of what we have grasped as true.

Recent documents of the episcopal magisterium and writings of theologians seem to be aware of this fact. Various documents of Vatican II,[14] hierarchical statements of many national episcopal conferences responding to *Humanae Vitae,*[15] and studies by Catholic theologians[16] have made it clear that a position of honest and responsible dissent from non-infallible teaching is legitimate. For example, the American hierarchy says this on the matter in their letter of 1968, "Human Life in Our Day":

> There exists in the Church a lawful freedom of inquiry and of thought and also general norms of licit dissent. This is particularly true in the area of legitimate theological speculation and research. When conclusions reached by such professional theological work prompt a scholar to dissent from non-infallible received teaching the norms of licit dissent come into play. They require of him careful respect for the consciences of those who lack his special competence or opportunity for judicious investigation. These norms also require setting forth his dissent with propriety and with regard for the gravity of the matter and the deference due the authority which has pronounced it.[17]

The discussions and clarifications of the right to dissent in recent years have helped to establish a new atmosphere for the pursuit of theological investigation and reinterpretations. These discussions have also shown that the significance of dissent as a source of new knowledge and reflection which can be used to enlighten and form our moral conscience is not in the *fact* of dissent as such, but in the *reasons*, the internal evidence, for the dissent. The reasonableness of the alternative position becomes the theological source of new knowledge for the formulation of conscience. This is right in line with the natural law tradition which has maintained that a moral conclusion is based on the reasons which support it, and not on the office of those who propose it.

Revisionist Theology and Probabilism

When the revisionist theologians point to the weightiness of the reasons for a moral position as constituting the theological source which the faithful might invoke in the formation of conscience, they find themselves in continuity with the tradition of probabilism in the Catholic Church.

Probabilism, as an accepted "moral system of conscience,"

dates back to the time of Alphonsus Liguori (1696–1787). Bernard Häring explains well how it came into prominence during the disputes of traditionalists and innovators of the sixteenth and seventeenth centuries. The "moral systems" of this time were concerned with the tensions between law, moral traditions, Church authorities, and pastoral guidance on the one hand, and the freedom of the individual conscience on the other. St. Alphonsus Liguori emerged with his interpretation of moderate probabilism to win the day against tutiorists (the "safer" position which contends that only an opinion clearly certain could be followed) and laxists (a position which contends that an opinion supported by even the slightest reasons could be followed).[18] The acceptable version of probabilism maintains that when there is widespread and presumably responsible theological opinion developing in the Church that opposes the traditionally accepted view, a person may legitimately take account of this new view in the formation of conscience.

Richard McCormick lands squarely within the tradition of probabilism with this statement:

> When a particular critique becomes one shared by many competent and demonstrably loyal scholars, it is part of the public opinion in the Church, a source of new knowledge and reflection. Surely this source of new knowledge and reflection cannot be excluded from those sources we draw upon to enlighten and form our consciences; for conscience is *formed within the Church.*[19]

Daniel Maguire, who advocates recovering probabilism for our day, praises it for " . . . [facing] the issue of what to do when moral consensus breaks down and a liberal opinion emerges saying that X, contrary to what all had thought, may be moral and good."[20]

Traditionally, what does it take for an opinion to be regarded as solidly probable? According to one of the standard moral manuals, an opinion could be regarded as "solidly probable" if it was not opposed to a "definition" of the Church and if it was based on reasons that are cogent though not necessarily conclusive (intrinsic probability) or by relying on the authority, learning, and prudence of other people (extrinsic probability).[21] In the tradition of probabilism, the opinions of reputable theologians had significance because these authorities created the presumption of reasonableness. The moral manual of Henry Davis summarizes it this way:

> Of course, the opinion of any chance theologian is not contemplated in this context as constituting a probable opinion, unless he is pre-eminent in his treatment of a given question; for when Probabilists speak of probable opinions, they define their own terms and these have to be accepted as they are defined. They define a probable opinion as that opinion to which a prudent man would give his assent, and they lay it down as fundamental to the system that a prudent man often does gives his assent to one of two contrary probable opinions, although he fully admits that there is a good deal to be said on the other side.[22]

Davis notes as well that for an opinion to be regarded as "probable" it does not require absolute certitude. There is room for contrary opinions in the system of probabilism. As Davis writes:

> Assent is necessarily given only to reasons that are evidently true, but probably true reasons never oblige the mind to assent, and consequently, when I act on the strength of a probable opinion, I am always conscious that though I am morally right in so acting, since I act prudently, nevertheless, the opinion of others who do not agree with me may be the true view of the case.[23]

While Häring, Maguire, and McCormick argue in defense of a renewed respect for the place of probabilism in the midst of moral pluralism, the use of probabilism does have its limitations today. Richard McCormick has acknowledged these limitations clearly in this statement:

> However, probabilism is not without its difficulties, difficulties inseparable from modifications in other areas of the-

ology. It is often difficult to determine what is a genuinely probably [sic] opinion, who is a reputable theological authority, and what weight is to be given to past and even present magisterial pronouncements. Furthermore, the very notion of a probable opinion on moral questions seems associated with an epistemology overly preoccupied with and confident of the achievement of a type of certainty that is frequently impossible. Chastened by history most reputable theologians have a renewed awareness of the depth and complexity of moral questions and prefer to grope, explore and question in an attempt to enlighten rather than to elaborate positions recognizable as "probable."[24]

Even with these limitations, the legitimate use of probabilism remains a tribute to human freedom. It is a solid ground in the Catholic tradition for giving revisionist theology a place of respect in the diversity of opinions in contemporary Catholic moral thought.

Revisionist Theology and the Moral Prohibitions of the Episcopal Moral Magisterium

Situating revisionist theology within the realm of a solidly probable opinion raises another concern for pastoral guidance. This is the concern of interpreting the moral prohibitions of the episcopal moral magisterium from the revisionist point of view and then using these interpretations in the formation of conscience. How would the revisionist approach to moral norms interpret the prohibitions of the episcopal magisterium expressed in material norms?

A brief restatement of the revisionist point of view on material norms helps address the question. Revisionist moral theologians regard material norms as necessarily conditioned formulations based on limited experience of conditioned values. Many values often conflict in the real world where moral choice is made. In this world of conflict, preference must be given to the greater values.

The revisionist point of view reads the material norms as general statements which light up premoral values and disvalues. The extent to which these premoral values must be actualized and the disvalues avoided in the individual cases depends on which values deserve preference when in relationship with concurring values. Louis Janssens puts it this way:

> . . . an action admitting or causing a premoral disvalue is morally right, when it serves a higher premoral value or safeguards the priority given to a lesser premoral disvalue. . . . In other words, we can have a proportionate reason to depart from the norm. Consequently concrete, material norms are relative in the sense of conditional. They are not binding, if there is a proportionate reason why the case at issue is not governed by them.[25]

Richard McCormick puts it this way:

> Such statements [i.e., magisterial statements of moral prohibitions] ought to be interpreted as general value judgments whose sense is: "This form of conduct represents a human deprivation, a disvalue and should be avoided insofar as is compatibly possible." ("Compatibly," s.c., with the other value co-present and conflicted.)[26]

These are two examples of how prominent revisionist theologians would interpret a moral prohibition of the episcopal magisterium that is expressed as a material norm. Richard McCormick goes on to say something very important about using this way of interpreting moral prohibitions of the episcopal magisterium in light of the way some moral documents of the episcopal magisterium are still being written:

> It is clear that this is not the way that a document like *Humanae Vitae* can be read, given the language use (*intrinsice inhonestum*) and the history of that language. But the argument is that this is the only supportable rendering of the prohibition. For otherwise the encyclical is taking the position that, regardless of the circumstances and other values co-present and in conflict, integral intercourse always is the greater (or more urgent) value deserving preference. But this conclusion has not been drawn by tradition about life

itself, a fact that makes it difficult, if not inconsistent, to draw it about a value less than life.[27]

In this light, pastoral guidance on *Humanae Vitae* based on a revisionist interpretation of moral norms would assert that the encyclical's basic message is that contraception is a disvalue which ought to be avoided insofar as is possible. To admit that something is a disvalue is to commit oneself to moving away from it as much as possible. Revisionist theologians tolerate actions causing disvalues only because more urgent values which deserve preference are at stake. McCormick puts this matter well in this paragraph which serves as a fitting conclusion to this section:

> This, I believe, is very important. Some reactions to *Humanae Vitae* framed the matter as follows: "contraception is wrong vs. contraception is right." This latter being the case since the argument for the former was seen as illegitimate. That is terribly misleading and, in my judgment, erroneous. It leaves the impression that contraception and sterilization are right, that nothing is wrong with them, and, eventually that they are values in themselves. When compared abstractly to their alternatives, contraception and sterilization are non-moral evils, what I call disvalues. To forget this is to lose the thrust away from their necessity. To say that something is a disvalue or non-moral evil is to imply thereby the need to be moving constantly and steadily to the point where causing of such disvalues is no longer required. To forget that something is a non-moral evil is to settle for it, to embrace it into one's world.[28]

Moral Norms and Moral Choice

In light of the above considerations, we can see that moral norms themselves do not determine the moral choice. Moral norms are the result of inferences from a wide range of human experiences; they illumine and guide moral choices, but do not definitively determine those choices without broader consultation. This in no way makes norms unimportant in the process of making a moral choice.

Because we have moral norms, we do not have to "invent the wheel" every time we make a moral decision. There is sufficient continuity in human experience to make these norms reliable guides for moral behavior. The more we are able to recognize that norms are inferences from the experience of value and necessarily conditioned by the limitations of knowledge and language, the more modest we will be in our claims about what norms can do about defining the moral order and determining our moral choices.

The revisionist understanding of moral norms in moral choice can be seen most clearly when contrasted with the manualist approach. The manuals represent an act-centered approach to morality and a norm-centered approach to decision-making. Norms are given a priority in a deductive process which is identified with the judgment of conscience. The manualist tradition reflects an approach to decision-making that takes a form something like this: The norm serves as the major premise of a syllogism, the minor premise is the situational analysis identifying the circumstances relevant to the norm, and the conclusion of this deductive process is the judgment of conscience. However, revisionist theologians are trying to show that complex moral reality cannot be captured adequately in the norm as a major premise, and that we can never fully analyze the situation to reduce it to a minor premise. The conclusion of any syllogism that we set up does not capture the unique, personal response of the moral agent. The revisionist approach to moral choice affirms the norms but understands that the moral choice is art as well as science; in other words, human situations are so complex that moral norms have to be applied imaginatively and wisely.[29] The moral choice can never be made independently of human persons and the complexity of human existence.

From the revisionist point of view, the moral choice seeks to actualize values. Values are primary; norms are secondary. Authentic moral living according to a properly informed conscience is neither a matter of stolidly fulfilling norms nor making an arbitrary and capricious response to each situation. Authentic moral living, rather, is the matter of actualizing values that deserve preference in a critical, responsible, and loving way. In order to determine which values deserve preference in a situation of conflict, there must be an assessment of the presence or absence of proportionate reason in the concrete circumstances. This assessment is the key to the revisionist use of norms in moral choice. In the revisionist approach, norms should not be forgotten as a component in pastoral guidance and in the formation of conscience. However, knowledge of norms alone does not equal an informed conscience. The proper assessment of proportionate reason involves a much broader base of consultation than turning to the norms alone.

In this light, simply to say "Let your conscience be your guide" as pastoral advice can be terribly misleading. This advice too easily suggests, "I can decide by myself," or "I can do whatever I feel is right," or even "Any reason will suffice as a proportionate reason." None of these are what revisionist theologians are saying.

The process of moral discernment which is implied by the revisionist approach—determining whether causing of disvalue is proportionately justified—is a demanding exercise. It demands at least the four considerations which James M. Gustafson has identified in his schema for moral discernment.[30] These are the four basic points that ought to be considered in any moral analysis addressing the practical moral question, "What should I do?"

The analysis begins and ends with the *moral agent*. Who is the "I" of "What should I do?" This involves clarifying the personal context of the moral agent by considering the person's capacities for certain moral action, the person's identity and integrity, as well as intentions. These considerations lead to the realm of *beliefs*, or stable convictions, which operate in a person's self-understanding and function to shape what the person sees as well as what the person considers possible to do. Beliefs also function to challenge the person to act in a way most consistent with the person's identity and integrity. Next, if morality is based on reality, then moral discernment demands getting a clear lay of the moral land. This involves *situational analysis*. Analyzing the situation involves exploring the reality-revealing questions as thoroughly as possible. A proper assessment of proportionate reason demands a clear knowledge of the circumstances which surround situations of conflict. Beyond analyzing the situation, moral discernment demands availing oneself of every source of moral wisdom available. This calls for a broad base of moral consultation appealing to *criteria of judgment*. Especially important at this stage is consulting the moral wisdom transmitted by the teaching of the Church and through the witness of the lives of moral virtuosos. Moral norms help tremendously in this process of consultation, for they are the generalized expressions of inference from a broad experience of value. But moral discernment does not stop with an appeal to moral wisdom, or moral norms. Discernment is not complete for the Christian moral person without bringing the full force of Christian beliefs and commitments to bear on the moral analysis as well as the evaluation and selection of viable alternatives for action. Exploring beliefs at this stage of discernment brings us back again close to the moral person who must decide and act. Figure 5 diagrams these component parts of moral discernment, and the arrow shows the movement of this discernment process. When Figure 5 is used in conjunction with Figure 3, we have a more complete view of what is involved in the moral discernment and strategy of decision-making according to a revisionist point of view.

This is indeed a demanding process. Moral norms have a significant place in this process, but moral norms can never effectively replace the broader consultation that makes up the discernment process for moral choice. Richard McCormick recognizes the risks involved in a process like this as well as the consequent need for broad moral consultation before making an authentic moral choice. His statement deserves repeating:

> This discernment process is full of risks, of personal leanings and self-interest and therefore it suggests *more* moral consultation and guidance than was called for when some of these norms were interpreted as proposing certain actions as inherently evil (in the traditional sense) and *never* justified.[31]

This approach to moral norms and moral choice realizes that the articulated wisdom of the moral community expressed in moral norms enlightens conscience, but never replaces conscience. The nature of a responsible moral decision excludes the notion of making any generalized formulation of value (that is, any moral norm) to be so particular as to substitute for the moral person's responsibility to choose.

While moral norms do not substitute for moral choice, moral norms continue to play a critical role in the moral life by pointing

Figure 5

COMPONENTS OF MORAL DISCERNMENT

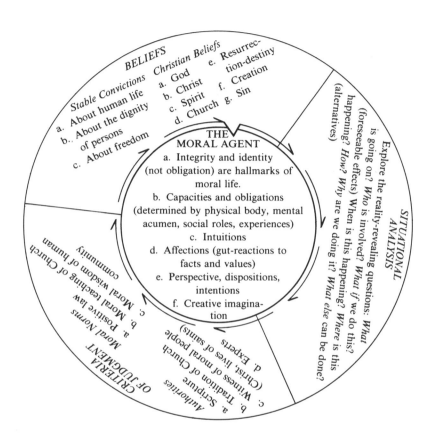

out values that humanize and disvalues which dehumanize. Louis Janssens stresses how the effort to formulate moral norms is an effort to bring the meaning and demands of the Great Commandment of love to our moral situations.[32] As expressions of the commandment of love, moral norms challenge us to move beyond the limitations which keep us from realizing a better humanity, to live up to the demands of love, and not to rest content with the limits of our situation.

Christ, the Norm of the Moral Life

Revisionist moral theology is clearly a person-centered approach to morality. A Christian approach to morality centered on persons and personal relationships must always begin and end with our relationship to God in Christ and through the Spirit. The first chapter indicated that a discussion of moral norms can easily seem to be far removed from the person of Christ and his moral message. Moral norms, however, are efforts to make meaningful the love which Jesus commanded in his moral message and embodied in himself. We have seen, too, that Christian moral discernment demands that we bring the full force of our Christian beliefs and commitments to bear on our interpretation of the moral situation and our selection of alternatives for moral action. It is fitting, then, that we end this little book as it began—with a focus on Christ. How do we look to Christ as the norm for the moral life?

Despite recent excellent work by biblical scholars on the moral teaching of Jesus in the New Testament, and despite recent thinking in Christology among systematic theologians, moral theologians, for the most part, have yet to undertake in a formal and full way the implications of Christology for the moral life. [33] (The Spirit has been even more neglected than Christ.) The question of Christ as moral norm is clearly bound up with the normative character of Scripture for morality and with the relationship and tension of faith and morality. These two issues set the agenda for a formal development of a Christology for morality. Since these issues have not been sufficiently explored, we can only make some preliminary reflections on the question of Christ as moral norm.

The Christian community claims to experience the presence of a

loving God reaching out to us in the midst of human life with compelling clarity in the person of Jesus Christ. This compelling clarity
gives Christ a unique authority for Christians. What makes Christ
the central moral norm is not any explicit moral teaching, but who
Jesus was and who he is as the Christ. In an insightful article, Donald P. Gray suggests that in Jesus we see God giving, man receiving,
and man giving what he has received.[34] These dynamic, interpersonal
categories of giving and receiving describe well what makes Christ
the central norm of the moral life—God giving himself in the fullest
way to humankind, and one from among humankind receiving and
giving himself in the fullest way to God. In short, Jesus as the Christ
expresses the fullness of what the Christian moral life ought to be.

To make such claims for Christ demands that we be guided in
our moral life by his person, word, and actions. For James M. Gustafson, who has written eloquently on the meaning of Christ as moral
norm, this means

> . . . to assume that what he means and symbolizes has au-
> thority for me, for example, that I am obliged to consider
> him both when there is a conformity of my own desire and
> preference with what he represents, and when he is abra-
> sive to my "natural" tendency on a particular occasion. . . .
> He is a standard by which my purposes are judged, he is an
> authority that ought to direct and inform my activity, if I
> acknowledge him to be my Lord.[35]

Gustafson says further that to remember Christ, and the significance
of his work, as part of making moral judgments in the Christian life
means this:

> . . . to recall him, and to think with reference to his deeds
> (including his death) and his words what trust in God's
> care and goodness and love for man required. It is some-
> times to have the imagination provoked by a parable, with
> the concreteness that that form of discourse has, and to ex-
> ercise one's imagination discerning what is concretely re-
> quired in the moment. It is sometimes to think analogically
> about the deeds we are given opportunity to do in relation

to the deeds Christ did under somewhat similar circumstances. It is sometimes to think very clearly about what the command of love requires, what an "in-principled love" or love in dialectic with equity, directs us to do in a given ambiguous instance. It is to be conformed to do what one discerns about Jesus' own attitude and bearing toward others, about the intentions that express and are shaped by his trust in God.[36]

Gustafson then makes only modest claims about what can be gained by making Christ a norm for the moral life. Making Christ the norm for the moral life does not guarantee moral superiority, nor does it assure one's sense of worth or salvation. What making Christ as norm does is this:

> Christ gives insight and direction; he shows something of the way in which his disciples are to follow. He helps them to see what options are more in conformity with the human good as it is understood in and through God's work and disclosure in him. He helps them to see what choices about ends to be sought and means to be used are in accord with trust in the goodness of God who gives and sustains life, and who acts to redeem it.[37]

This description of Christ as norm, the source of illumination for the moral life, puts the matter about as well as it can be put in the present state of the discussion.

Discipleship, following Christ, is what is at the heart of claiming Christ as the norm of the moral life. We number ourselves among generations of Christians who have found most compelling in Jesus the fact that he was one of us. He is one who has known our pain and our joy and reveals our deepest possibilities. Jesus lived his life with his heart set on one thing—the Father and his kingdom. The core of the mission of Jesus was to proclaim the kingdom of God. The teaching of Jesus is dominated by the urgency to proclaim the kingdom of forgiveness, healing, justice, and freedom. We distort the message of Jesus, his teaching and his person if we remove him so far from our life that we cannot follow him. The Jesus of the Gospels is a man who tested life, was tested by life, and searched out life's meaning by listening carefully to what makes life really valuable, and then decided for the Father's kingdom.

Jesus continues to call us to those values and decisions. He calls us not as one who does not know our humanity, but as one who lived the human adventure from within and challenges us to take the same path that leads to resurrection. Jesus lived his life trusting that life was not a bad joke. He died his death believing that his words and deeds would not echo into an empty future. He invites us to do the same. This is the challenge of being a disciple. This is the challenge of the "imitation" of Christ. It is not the challenge to see if we could mimic Jesus, a first-century Palestinian Jew. Rather, it is the challenge to live our human adventure as authentically as he lived his.

The potential of our discipleship for resolving moral difficulties in concrete cases is not without problems. Our capacities for commitment and our degrees of commitment are significantly influential factors. Yet, the value of discipleship is that it inspires a vision and provides a context for all moral analysis and moral choice.

Notes

1. Richard A. McCormick has addressed each of the points of criticism considered here to a greater or less extent in his "Moral Notes" in *Theological Studies* since 1972. See also his response to comments on his *Ambiguity in Moral Choice* in his essay "A Commentary on the Commentaries," in *Doing Evil*, pp. 193–267.

2. "The Moral Meaning of Human Acts," *Homiletic and Pastoral Review* 79 (October 1978): 14.

3. *Health Care Ethics* (St. Louis: The Catholic Hospital Association, 1978), pp. 190–191.

4. "Morality of Consequences: A Critical Appraisal," in *Readings in Moral Theology No. 1,* p. 246. See also his most recent criticism in "Catholic Ethics: Has the Norm for Rule-Making Changed?" *Theological Studies* 42 (June 1981): 232–250.

5. "Morality of Consequences: A Critical Appraisal," in *Readings in Moral Theology No. 1,* p. 257.

6. *Health Care Ethics,* p. 191

7. "The Moral Meaning of Human Acts," *Homiletic and Pastoral Review,* p.13.

8. "Morality by Calculation of Values," in *Readings in Moral Theology No. 1*, pp. 271–275.

9. *Ibid.*, p. 275.

10. *Abortion*, p. 310. He repeats his criticism in a book co-authored with Joseph N. Boyle, Jr., *Life and Death with Liberty and Justice* (Notre Dame: University of Notre Dame Press, 1979), see pp. 348–355; almost identical quote is found on p. 352. For Paul Ramsey's criticism of this dimension of the revisionist approach, see his commentary on McCormick's *Ambiguity in Moral Choice* in his "Incommensurability and Indeterminancy in Moral Choice," in *Doing Evil*, pp. 69–144.

11. The relevant quotation of Pius XII is this: "But if the Supreme Pontiffs in their official documents purposely pass judgment on a matter up to that time under dispute, it is obvious that that matter, according to the mind and will of the same Pontiffs, cannot be any longer considered a question open to discussion among theologians": *AAS*, Vol. 42 (1950), p. 568.

12. For only a few of the many studies on this issue, see the following: Avery Dulles, "The Theologian and the Magisterium," *CTSA Proceedings* 31 (1976): 235–246; revised as "Doctrinal Authority for a Pilgrim Church," in *The Resilient Church* (Garden City: Doubleday, 1976), pp. 93–112; Joseph A. Komonchak, "Ordinary Papal Magisterium and Religious Assent," in *Contraception: Authority and Dissent*, ed. Charles E. Curran (New York: Herder and Herder, 1969), pp. 101–126; also Komonchak, "*Humanae Vitae* and Its Reception: Ecclesiological Reflections," *Theological Studies* 39 (June 1978): 221–257; Richard A. McCormick, "Moral Notes," *Theological Studies* 29 (December 1969): 644–648; 37 (March 1976): 70–119; 38 (March 1977): 57–114; 40 (March 1979): 59–112; McCormick, "The Teaching of the Magisterium and the Theologians," *CTSA Proceedings* 24 (1969): 234–254; also, McCormick, "Authority and Morality," *America* 142 (March 1, 1980): 169–171; K. O'Reilly, "The Roman Catholic Magisterium and Legitimate Dissent," in *Authority, Conscience and Dissent* (New Zealand: The National Council of Churches, 1971), pp. 124–163; Karl Rahner, "The Teaching Office of the Church in the Present-Day Crisis of Authority," *Theological Investigations*, Vol. XII, translated by David Bourke (New York: Seabury Press, 1974), pp. 3–30.

13. Richard McCormick, "Personal Conscience," *An American Catholic Catechism*, edited by George J. Dyer (New York: Seabury Press, 1975), pp. 184–185. For a more complete statement of the response due the ordinary magisterium in moral matters, see McCormick's "Moral Notes," *Theological Studies* 29 (December 1968): 716–718, and 30 (December 1969): 651–653.

14. *LG*, nn. 4, 12, 52, 37; *GS*, nn.16, 62, 92; *DH*, n. 14; *AG*, nn. 4, 23.

15. For a summary of many of these responses, see William H. Shannon, *The Lively Debate* (New York: Sheed and Ward, 1970), pp. 117–146.

16. See note 12 above.

17. As found in the collection of official Church documents, *Love and Sexuality*, edited by Liebard, p. 366.

18. Bernard Häring, *Free and Faithful in Christ*, Vol. 1 *General Moral Theology*, pp. 284–290.

19. "Moral Notes," *Theological Studies* 40 (March 1979): 96–97; cf. "Personal Conscience," *An American Catholic Catechism*, p. 187.

20. "Catholic Ethics," *America in Theological Perspective*, edited by Thomas M. McFadden (New York: Seabury Press, 1976), p. 26. Maguire has repeated his advocacy for probabilism in "*Human Sexuality:* The Book and the Epiphenomenon," *CTSA Proceedings* 33 (1978): 54–76, esp. pp. 71–76; this last article is reprinted as "Of Sex and Ethical Methodology" in *Dimensions of Human Sexuality*, edited by Dennis Doherty (Garden City: Doubleday, 1979), pp. 125–148.

21. H. Noldin, A. Schmitt, G. Heinzel, *Summa Theologiae Moralis*, Vol. 1 *De Principiis*, thirtieth edition (Innsbruck: Felizian Rauch, 1952), p. 218. Cf. Henry Davis, *Moral and Pastoral Theology*, Vol. 1 *Human Acts, Law, Sin, Virtue* (London: Sheed and Ward, 1945), p. 95.

22. Davis, *Moral and Pastoral Theology*, Vol. 1, p. 95.

23. *Ibid.*, p. 107.

24. "Personal Conscience," *An American Catholic Catechism*, pp. 188–189.

25. "Norms and Priorities in a Love Ethics," p. 217.

26. "Moral Norms and Their Meaning," *Lectureship*, p. 44.

27. *Ibid.*

28. *Ibid.*, p. 45, cf. "Moral Notes," *Theological Studies* 40 (March 1979): 86.

29. For a fine statement of the "art" as well as "science" dimension of moral choice, see Daniel C. Maguire, *The Moral Choice*, pp. 110–112.

30. Gustafson's four elements which form the framework for moral discernment can be found in "Moral Discernment in the Christian Life," *Theology and Christian Ethics*, pp. 99–119; "Context Versus Principles: A Misplaced Debate in Christian Ethics," *Christian Ethics and the Community*, pp. 101–126; and "The Relationship of Empirical Science to Moral Thought," *Theology and Christian Ethics*, pp. 215–228. For the way in which these four elements constitute the moral level of discourse and relate to the three formal elements of the level of ethical discourse, see Figure 1 in Chapter One above.

31. "Moral Norms and Their Meaning," *Lectureship*, p. 46.

32. See especially, "Norms and Priorities in a Love Ethics."

33. A very notable exception is James M. Gustafson, *Christ and the Moral Life*. Gustafson is not in dialogue with contemporary efforts in Christology, but uses some classical positions. For an effort that tries to draw out implications for morality of contemporary efforts in Christology, see Jon Sobrino, *Christology at the Crossroads,* translated by John Drury (Maryknoll: Orbis Books, 1978); see especially the section "Jesus' Faith and Fundamental Moral Theology," pp. 108–139.

34. "The Incarnation: God's Giving and Man's Receiving," *Horizon* 1 (Fall 1974): 1–113.

35. *Christ and the Moral Life*, pp. 264–265.

36. *Ibid.*, p. 269.

37. *Ibid.*, pp. 269–270.

Appendix

If you have read this far, you may be wondering how to evaluate what theologians are saying about moral norms. How are we to regard these theological opinions when the episcopal magisterium has already spoken clearly on so many moral matters? Is not the voice of the Pope or the bishops enough? Why do we need to give attention to what the theologians are saying? If we do, then what is the relationship of these theological opinions to the normative teaching of the Pope and the bishops? Is the general direction in which many contemporary moral theologians are moving compatible with positions taken in official Church documents?

These are common questions. These are good questions. These are questions many people ask who are confused by so many theological opinions that do not seem to square with what they understand the official Church to be saying. Since this book was primarily a work of exposition and limited to what theologians are saying, this Appendix seems to be an appropriate addition in order to provide a proper forum in which to cite pertinent documentation with which to evaluate the directions of this yet incomplete discussion of moral norms. Is what theologians are saying to be read as subtle movements against authoritative teaching? Or is the general direction of the investigations and interpretations the theologians are making within the perimeters of official Church teaching?

Of the many issues at stake in answering these questions, two seem to be crucial for evaluating what the theologians are saying in light of official Church teaching. One crucial issue is the matter of carrying on theological investigations and interpretations from the perspective of the historical consciousness so characteristic of the modern worldview. The other issue is the relationship between the papal and episcopal magisterium and theologians.

Historical Consciousness

Chapter Two provided a brief sketch of the modern worldview and historical consciousness. There we saw that historical consciousness recognizes that every thought-system and language is conditioned by time and culture. This means that not only the formulations of the theologians but also those of the episcopal magisterium are necessarily limited.

There is a growing awareness and official recognition on the part of the episcopal magisterium that historical consciousness can and must be recognized as a factor in formulating and interpreting official teachings of the Church. The official documents which endorsed and encouraged the biblical renewal in the Roman Catholic Church show evidence of this. Here we recall *Divino Afflante Spiritu* (1943), the Instruction of the Pontifical Biblical Comission, "The Historical Truth of the Gospels" (1964), and Vatican II's *Dogmatic Constitution on Divine Revelation* (1965). Through these documents the Church recognizes that the books of the Bible contain the word of God in the limited words of men and women of various ages. To discover God's revelation we must take into account the historical situation, the philosophical worldview, and the theological limitations of those who wrote these books. The same limiting conditions which affect the Bible, its composition and its interpretation also affect the dogmas and moral teachings of the Church.

We can find the glimmering of an official acknowledgement of historical conditioning in the speech with which Pope John XXIII opened the Vatican Council (October 11, 1962). There the Holy Father distinguished between the substance of a teaching and its formulation: "The substance of the ancient doctrine of the deposit of faith is one thing, and the way it is presented is another."[1] This same insight is clearly affirmed and pursued at length a decade later in *Mysterium Ecclesiae* (1973), a declaration of the Doctrinal Congregation.

This document accepts the principle of historical conditioning of the formulations of Church teachings. What this document says about interpreting statements pertaining to dogma can be said about statements in morality as well. Since this document is of such central importance, it is worth quoting the text at length. This following selection is the translation of the NC News Service Documentary but I have added italics and numbered paragraph divisions:

The transmission of divine revelation by the Church encounters difficulties of various kinds. These arise from the fact that the hidden mysteries of God "by their nature so far transcend the human intellect that even if they are revealed to us and accepted by faith, they remain concealed by the veil of faith itself and are, as it were, wrapped in darkness" (Vatican I). *Difficulties also arise from the historical condition that affects the expression of revelation.*

(1) With regard to this historical condition, it must first be observed that *the meaning of the pronouncement of faith depends partly on the expressive power of the language used* at a certain point in time and in particular circumstances.

(2) Moreover, it sometimes happens that some dogmatic truth is *first expressed incompletely* (but not falsely), and at a later date, when considered in a broader context of faith or human knowledge, it receives a fuller and more perfect expression.

(3) In addition, when the Church makes new pronouncements, she intends to confirm or clarify what is in some way contained in Sacred Scripture or in previous expressions of tradition. But at the same time she usually has the intention of *solving certain questions* or removing certain errors. All these things have to be taken into account in order that these pronouncements may be properly interpreted.

(4) Finally, even though the truths which the Church intends to teach through her dogmatic formulas are distinct

from *the changeable conceptions of a given epoch* and can be expressed without them, nevertheless, it can sometimes happen that these truths may be enunciated by the sacred magisterium *in terms that bear the traces of such conceptions.*

In view of the above, it must be stated that the dogmatic formulas of the Church's magisterium were from the very beginning suitable for communicating revealed truth, and that as they are, they remain forever suitable for communicating this truth to those who interpret them correctly. *It does not follow, however, that every one of these formulas has always been [suitable for communicating truth] or will always be so to the same extent.* For this reason theologians seek to define exactly the intention of teaching proper to the various formulas, and in carrying out this work they are of considerable assistance to the living magisterium of the Church, to which they remain subordinated. For this reason also it often happens that ancient dogmatic formulas and others closely connected with them remain living and fruitful in the habitual usage of the Church, but with suitable expository and explanatory additions that maintain and clarify their original meaning. In addition, it has sometimes happened that in this habitual usage of the Church *certain of these formulas gave way to new expressions which,* proposed and approved by the sacred magisterium, *presented more clearly or more completely the same meaning.*

As for the *meaning* of dogmatic formulas, this remains ever true and constant in the Church, even when it is expressed with greater clarity or more developed. The faithful therefore must shun the opinion, first, that dogmatic formulas (or some category of them) cannot signify truth in a determinate way, but can offer only changeable approximations to it, which to a certain extent distort or alter it; secondly, that these formulas signify the truth only in an indeterminate way, this truth being like a goal that is constantly being sought by means of such approximations. Those who hold such an opinion do not avoid dogmatic relativism, and they corrupt the concept of the Church's infallibility relative to the truth to be taught or held in a determinate way.[2]

Many of the contemporary theologians represented in this book work in the light of the principles of interpretation found here.

The Relationship Between the Episcopal Magisterium and the Theologians

Once we recognize that every thought-system and language is inevitably limited, we can appreciate the need for cooperation, collaboration, and collegial association of the papal and episcopal magisterium and all people of good will searching for truth. The documents of Vatican II remain a remarkable case in point of what can happen when this collaboration takes place. The experience of Vatican II teaches us that the formulation of the substance of faith and morals is very much a teaching-learning *process.*

In this process, the episcopal magisterium is an indispensable vehicle for preserving past insights into revealed truth and for formulating those insights. The episcopal magisterium is also a precious vehicle for gathering, evaluating, and promulgating our shared experience and knowledge in order authoritatively to defend the Catholic integrity and unity of faith and morals. The International Theological Commission's "Theses on the Relationship Between the Ecclesiastical Magisterium and Theology" captures well the specific functions of the ecclesiastical magisterium this way:

> These are: "the task of authoritatively interpreting the word of God, written and handed-down," the censuring of opinions which endanger the faith and morals proper to the Church, the proposing of truths which are of particular contemporary relevance. Although it is not the work of the magisterium to propose theological syntheses, still, because of its concern for unity, it must consider individual truths in the light of the whole, since integrating a particular truth into the whole belongs to the very nature of truth.[3]

In fulfilling these functions, the episcopal magisterium exercises its pastoral responsibility. In moral matters this pastoral responsibility is carried out by making prudential determinations of the relation of basic principles to changing times. As times change, the prudential determination of the application of abiding principles may change. This possibility is clearly manifest in the development of Catholic social ethics as the difference in nuance between *Rerum Novarum* and *Populorum Progressio* illustrates so well.

For the episcopal magisterium to carry out its pastoral responsibilities in moral matters, it draws upon theological reflection. Every doctrinal and moral formulation that comes from the Pope or bishops is based on the research and reflection of theologians. Theology mediates between the Pope and bishops and the community of believers by not only showing how the teaching of the papal and episcopal magisterium is rooted in Scripture and tradition, but also by carrying on the work of interpreting this teaching and translating it into a contemporary mode. The theologians assist the Pope and the bishops by fulfilling their responsibility of understanding the experience of the Church as reflected in its documents and in the ongoing life of the people of God.

In Catholic theology, the magisterium of the Pope and bishops is not "just another voice" in the Catholic community. For this reason, Vatican II's *Declaration on Religious Freedom* clearly says, "In the formation of their conscience, the Christian faithful ought carefully to attend to the sacred and certain doctrine of the Church" (n. 14). The American bishops' pastoral reflection on the moral life, "To Live in Christ Jesus," repeats this statement of the *Declaration on Religious Freedom* and then adds, "The authoritative moral teachings of the Church enlighten personal conscience and are to be regarded as certain and binding norms of morality."[4] Most recently, the national catechetical directory, *Sharing the Light of Faith*, says that Catholics "should always measure their moral judgments by the magisterium," and it adds: "When faced with questions which pertain to dissent from non-infallible teachings of the Church, it is important for catechists to keep in mind that the presumption is always in favor of the magisterium."[5] Chapter Five showed the way theologians interpret the "presumption" that ought to be given non-infallible teaching, the response due such teaching, and the significant place the teachings of the Church ought to have in the formation of conscience.

In Catholic theology, the episcopal magisterium is gifted by God with a special charism to teach and to speak with authority.

> The magisterium derives its authority from sacramental or-dination which "along with the task of sanctifying confers also the tasks of teaching and ruling." This "formal author-ity," as it is called, is at once charismatic and juridical, and it founds the right and the duty of the magisterium insofar as it is a share in the authority of Christ.[6]

Given this privileged place and this authority does not mean that the teaching of the magisterium can never be broadened, deepened, or modified (cf. the teaching on religious freedom). The task to grasp the truth of the Gospel is an ongoing struggle. We all share in that struggle in different ways. As the American hierarchy's pastoral let-ter on the moral life says:

> There are many instruments and agents of teaching in the Church. All have roles in drawing out the richness of Christ's message and proclaiming it, each according to his or her gift. Although we cannot discuss their role at length here, we wish in particular to acknowledge and encourage the contributions which theologians make to this effort.[7]

In struggling to understand the richness of Christ's message, ongoing Christian experience, or the teachings of the Pope and bishops, theo-logians are not setting themselves above the Pope or the bishops. Ide-ally, theologians are collaborating with them in a joint effort to understand what God is saying to us and what God would want of us.

Conclusion

This book has surveyed a fairly good sample of the significant contributions that theologians are making to the issue of moral norms as part of their role in this collaborative process of coming to clearer formulations of moral teaching. The two issues, historical consciousness and the relation of theologians to the ecclesiastical magisterium, serve as the larger context in which to evaluate the general directions of what theologians are saying in light of official Church teaching. The Church has accepted the principle of historical conditioning of formulations of the substance of faith and morals, and the Church recognizes and encourages cooperation and collaboration between the papal and episcopal magisterium and theologians. The theologians share with the Pope and bishops the common task of teaching, but with different authority and responsibility.

Notes

1. Walter M. Abbott, ed., *The Documents of Vatican II* (New York: The America Press, 1966), p. 715. For a similar statement in a Council document, see *Pastoral Constitution on the Church in the Modern World*, n. 62.

2. *AAS* 65 (1973), pp. 402–404.

3. *Theses* issued June 6, 1976 (Washington: USCC Publications Office, 1977), p. 4.

4. Washington: USCC Publications Office, 1976, p. 12.

5. Washington: USCC Publications Office, 1979, n.190, p. 114.

6. International Theological Commission, *Theses,* p. 5.

7. "To Live in Christ Jesus," p.12.

Suggestions for Further Reading

The following suggested readings are divided by chapter, according to the main issues raised in each chapter.

Chapter One: Moral Norms and Moral Theology

A still valuable book for understanding the moral message of Jesus is Rudolf Schnackenburg, *The Moral Teaching of the New Testament* (New York: Herder and Herder, 1965). On the theme of "love" in the New Testament, see especially Victor Paul Furnish, *The Love Commandment in the New Testament* (Nashville: Abingdon Press, 1972).

James M. Gustafson has been quite explicit about the structure of Christian ethics and the formal elements that constitute the range of interest in moral theology. For two brief pertinent articles on this matter see, in the collection *Christian Ethics and the Community* (Philadelphia: United Church Press, 1971), "Theology and Ethics," pp. 83–100, and "Context Versus Principles: A Misplaced Debate in Christian Ethics," pp. 101–126. For two books that illustrate the formal elements in moral theology, see *Christ and the Moral Life* (New York: Harper and Row, 1968) and *Can Ethics Be Christian?* (Chicago: University of Chicago Press, 1975).

Chapter Two: The New Context for Moral Norms

The most helpful contributions to understanding the new context for theology today have been made by Bernard Lonergan. See, for example, "Theology in Its New Context," in *Theology of Renewal, Vol. 1: Renewal of Religious Thought*, edited by L. K. Shook (New York: Herder and Herder, 1968), pp. 34–46; "Dimensions of Meaning," in *Collection*, edited by F. E. Crowe (New York: Herder and Herder, 1967), pp. 221–239; and *Method in Theology* (New York: Herder and Herder, 1972).

Chapter Three: The Sources of Moral Norms

The use of Scripture as a source of moral norms is an area that has received some preliminary attention but needs further development. For a seminal work in this area, see the book co-authored by a biblical scholar and an ethician, Bruce C. Birch and Larry L. Rasmussen, *Bible and Ethics in the Christian Life* (Minneapolis: Augsburg Publishing House, 1976). For two articles, see Charles E. Curran, "Dialogue with the Scriptures: The Role and Function of the Scriptures in Moral Theology," *Catholic Moral Theology in Dialogue* (Notre Dame: Fides Publishers, 1972), pp. 24–64; and James M. Gustafson, "The Place of Scripture in Christian Ethics: A Methodological Study," *Theology and Christian Ethics* (Philadelphia: United Church Press, 1974), pp. 121–145.

The literature on natural law is vast. Josef Fuchs' *Natural Law*, translated by Helmut Rickter and John A. Dowling (New York: Sheed and Ward, 1965), is still valuable though very difficult to read. A still valuable collection of essays on the topic is the one by Charles E. Curran, David Little, Bernard Häring, John G. Milhaven, and Richard A. McCormick in "Part Two—Natural Law: A Reassessment of the Tradition," in *Norm and Context in Christian Ethics*, edited by Gene H. Outka and Paul Ramsey (New York: Charles Scribner's Sons, 1968). A brief essay that pulls together well much of the discussion on natural law is by Edward A. Malloy, "Natural Law Theory and Catholic Moral Theology," *American Ecclesiastical Review* 169 (September 1975): 456–469. George M. Regan's chapter "Natural Law in the Christian Life" in *New Trends in Moral Theol-*

ogy (New York: Newman Press, 1971), pp. 115–144, is still valuable. More recently, a valuable summary of recent literature on natural law has been provided by Timothy E. O'Connell in "Part Three" of *Principles for a Catholic Morality* (New York: The Seabury Press, 1978), pp. 117–195.

Chapter Four: The Meaning and Limits of Moral Norms

For a brief discussion of the importance of formal norms, see Timothy E. O'Connell, "The Question of Moral Norms," *American Ecclesiastical Review* 169 (June 1975): 377–388.

The strict consequentialist position is best represented in the literature of Joseph Fletcher. See his celebrated *Situation Ethics: The New Morality* (Philadelphia: The Westminster Press, 1966). This book has been much discussed. For only two collections of essays discussing "situation ethics," see *The Situation Ethics Debate*, edited by Harvey Cox (Philadelphia: The Westminster Press, 1968) and *Storm Over Ethics*, John C. Bennett, *et al.* (Philadelphia: United Church Press, 1967).

The mixed consequentialism of revisionist Catholic theology is well represented in the collection of essays *Readings in Moral Theology No. 1: Moral Norms and Catholic Tradition*, edited by Charles E. Curran and Richard A. McCormick (New York: Paulist Press, 1979).

The deontological approach is represented by Germain Grisez, *Abortion: The Myths, the Realities, and the Arguments* (New York: Corpus Books, 1970) and William E. May, *Becoming Human* (Dayton: Pflaum Publishing Co., 1975). Paul Ramsey's approach is represented in his writings which are quite vast and wide-ranging. For some good examples of his deontological approach, see his early work, *Basic Christian Ethics* (New York: Charles Scribner's Sons, 1950) and his response to situation ethics in *Deeds and Rules in Christian Ethics* (New York: Charles Scribner's Sons, 1967).

Chapter Five: Moral Norms and Pastoral Guidance

The important practical implications of the revisionist approach to moral norms is represented by Richard A. McCormick, "Personal

Conscience," in *An American Catholic Catechism*, edited by George Dyer (New York: Seabury Press, 1975), pp. 181–193. Also valuable for a more complete view of the revisionist approach at work, see Daniel C. Maguire, *The Moral Choice* (Garden City: Doubleday, 1978); see also Bernard Häring, *Free and Faithful in Christ, Vol. 1: General Moral Theology* (New York: The Seabury Press, 1978).